CHILD LABOR AND SWEATSHOPS

Other Books in the At Issue Series:

CHILD LABOR AND SWEATSHOPS

Mary E. Williams, *Book Editor*

David Bender, *Publisher*
Bruno Leone, *Executive Editor*

Bonnie Szumski, *Editorial Director*
Brenda Stalcup, *Managing Editor*
Scott Barbour, *Senior Editor*

An Opposing Viewpoints® Series

Greenhaven Press, Inc.
San Diego, California

Library of Congress Cataloging-in-Publication Data

Child labor and sweatshops / Mary E. Williams, book editor.
        p.   cm. — (At issue) (An opposing viewpoints series)
    Includes bibliographical references and index.
    ISBN 0-7377-0002-5 (pbk. : alk. paper). —
ISBN 0-7377-0003-3 (lib. : alk. paper)
    1. Children—Employment. 2. Sweatshops. I. Williams, Mary E.,
1960– . II. Series: At issue (San Diego, Calif.) III. Series:
Opposing viewpoints series (Unnumbered)
HD6231.C455   1999
331.3'1—DC21   98-11685
                                                                          CIP

©1999 by Greenhaven Press, Inc., PO Box 289009,
San Diego, CA 92198-9009

Printed in the U.S.A.

Table of Contents

Introduction

When he was four years old, Iqbal Masih was sold into bonded servitude by his parents, a common practice of poor Pakistani families hoping to pay off debts owed to landlords and local merchants. For the next six years, Masih was forced to work in a carpet factory—usually chained to a loom—for up to sixteen hours a day, six days a week. A small, sickly boy, Masih's growth was further stunted by malnutrition, carpet dust, constant stooping, and beatings he received as punishment for his repeated escape attempts and occasional refusal to work. At the age of ten, however, Masih saw posters distributed by the Bonded Labor Liberation Front (BLLF), a human rights organization founded by labor activist Ehsan Khan. These posters revealed that bonded and child labor were illegal in Pakistan—a fact generally ignored by the local manufacturers and civil officials. Masih secretly contacted BLLF members, who helped him escape from the carpet factory. Soon afterwards, Masih joined the BLLF and worked with them to liberate 3,000 bonded children from textile, brick, and steel factories in Pakistan.

Under the tutelage of Ehsan Khan, Masih became a spokesman for the bonded children of south Asia, and he traveled to the United States and Europe to persuade potential buyers to stop purchasing Pakistani carpets until the country enforced its child labor laws. In 1992, as a result of Masih's efforts, Pakistan's carpet sales fell for the first time in twenty years. The boy's success gained international attention, and in 1994, he won the Reebok Human Rights Youth in Action Award and a future scholarship to an American university. In 1995, however, twelve-year-old Masih was shot to death while visiting relatives in a rural village. Khan maintains that Masih was assassinated by the "carpet mafia"—members of the Pakistan Carpet Manufacturers and Exporters Association who were eager to keep child laborers in their factories.

Iqbal Masih's life and violent death have inspired many organizations, consumer groups, businesses, and individuals to contest the use of child labor. Canadian Craig Kielburger was twelve when he learned of Iqbal's story and began researching the issue of working children. In an article printed in the December 15, 1996, *Chicago Tribune*, Kielburger states that before reading about Masih, "I did not know very much about where my running shoes or soccer balls were made, or who made them. . . . Poor children in many countries are employed in the textile, sporting goods and toy industries, making products that may eventually end up on the shelves of North American stores. By buying these products, we may be contributing to the exploitation of children." With a group of friends, Kielburger launched Free the Children, an organization that urges consumers to learn about the origin and assembly of goods and to buy child-labor-free products. Kielburger has taken personally funded tours of factories in several Asian countries to investigate the working conditions of child laborers, and Free the Children has initiated letter-writing campaigns and petitions urging businesses and governments to eliminate the use of child labor.

Many advocates for children argue that efforts such as Kielburger's are desperately needed because most child laborers work under abusive and horrific conditions. These workers often toil for twelve to eighteen hours a day in congested, dusty, dangerous environments that severely impair their health, activists contend. Some child laborers, advocates point out, face verbal, physical, and even sexual abuse from their bosses. Since most of them do not obtain an education, child workers cannot attain higher-paying jobs as adults and stay trapped in poverty all of their lives, activists maintain. According to the International Labour Organization, a workers' rights alliance, there are at least 250 million workers between the ages of five and fourteen in third world countries. This number may be as high as 500 million—half of the children in the developing world—if undeclared workers and domestic workers are included. For these reasons, asserts Kielburger, "we . . . have to push for education, protection, and the rights of the child."

In addition to Kielburger's Free the Children campaign, concerned parties have taken several other measures in an attempt to stop the exploitation of child labor. In 1992, Democratic senator Tom Harkin first introduced the Child Labor Deterrence Act, a congressional bill that proposes a ban on the importation of products made by children overseas. Harkin argues that this legislation endeavors "to stop the economic exploitation of children and to get them out of the most dangerous jobs . . . by limiting the role of the U.S. in providing an open market for foreign goods made by underage kids." As of November 1998, Harkin's legislation had not passed. However, some North American locales—such as Bangor, Maine, and North Olmsted, Ohio—have instituted their own voluntary boycotts by passing ordinances prohibiting the purchase of goods made by sweatshop and child labor. Moreover, several companies, including Levi Strauss, Guess, and The Gap, have recently adopted a "No Sweat" policy that ensures that their stores do not carry products made by suppliers that exploit children or adult workers.

Other activists have taken a different route by implementing labeling programs that ensure that a specific product has been made without the use of child labor. Child advocate Kailash Satyarthi, for example, established Rugmark, a nonprofit foundation that allows consumers to identify hand-knotted rugs made only by adult labor. Rugmark inspects factories that wish to be certified as child-labor free and attaches special Rugmark labels to carpets that meet their requirements. Through these kinds of actions, many human rights activists hope to stop the abuse and exploitation of child laborers. "To do less with the knowledge that we have today on the extent of this problem is to be a coexploiter of children," insists California state representative George Miller.

Some activists caution, however, that humanitarian challenges to the use of child labor can backfire. For example, 50,000 Bangladeshi children garment workers lost their jobs in 1994 after news of Harkin's Child Labor Deterrence bill aired. Many of these children then took on the more dangerous work of stone crushing or prostitution to make ends meet. According to Bangladeshi writer and activist Shahidul Alam, children factory workers in third world countries contribute needed income to their households, and if these children are forced to leave their jobs they must choose between a life of increased poverty or a life of more exploitative, and often illegal, work. "Childhood [in Bangladesh] is seen as a period for learning employable skills," writes Alam. "Children have always helped out with family duties. When this evolves into a paid job . . . neither children nor their families see it as anything unusual. In poor families it is simply understood that everyone has to work." Alam contends that the complexity of the child labor issue must be reexamined if human rights activists truly want to improve the lives of working children.

To avoid scenarios such as the one in Bangladesh, many activist organizations do not support the boycott of goods made by children. Instead, they demand safe and humane working conditions for children along with a serious examination of the socioeconomic conditions that require young children to work. At the first international conference of child laborers held in 1996 in Kundapur, India, child delegates from thirty-three developing countries drafted a ten-point proposal that rejected the tactic of boycotts and called for "work with dignity, with hours adapted so that we have time for education and leisure." They also requested opportunities for professional training, access to good health care, and more actions that would address "the root causes of our situation, primarily poverty."

While human rights activists may disagree about the best approaches to ending the exploitation of working children, some analysts contend that Westerners should maintain a "hands off" stance toward child labor in the developing world. For one thing, critics argue, labeling programs such as Rugmark's are probably futile. Rugmark uses only eighteen inspectors to examine more than eighteen thousand looms, and, in the opinion of Columbia University professor Elliott Schrage, "Without a video camera on every loom in every home where rugs are made, there's no way you can know if children were involved." Moreover, critics point out, inspectors could simply be bribed to lie about the use of child labor. Instead of trying to force overseas manufacturers to abide by seemingly more enlightened labor standards, argues economist Murray Weidenbaum, Western consumers should recognize that the use of child labor and low-wage workers is a natural stage in the industrial development of poor nations. As nations become more economically successful, Weidenbaum contends, they generally abandon exploitative labor practices. Such was the case for many national economies of the twentieth century, he points out: "Japan moved from poverty to wealth, as did South Korea in the last half of the twentieth century. . . . Nations in Southeast Asia are undergoing a similar transformation. In each of these cases, rising portions of the population advanced to better paying jobs—not as a result of idealism but from changing economic circumstances."

Concerns about the use of child labor and sweatshops are likely to increase as corporate power continues to expand into multinational domains and as a growing number of companies come to rely on outside manufacturers. Child laborers, of course, are not the only ones who are exploited. Adult workers in many third world countries—and even in the United States—face long hours, menial pay, and hazardous working conditions. The authors in *At Issue: Child Labor and Sweatshops* examine the issues surrounding the use of child laborers and adult workers who are exposed to substandard work environments.

1

Child Labor and Sweatshops: An Overview

Charles S. Clark

Charles S. Clark is a former staff writer for CQ Researcher, *a weekly report on current social issues.*

Concern about the use of child labor and sweatshops has grown as retailers in industrialized nations have increasingly come to rely on low-wage workers—often people in developing nations—to produce goods. Labor leaders and human rights activists point out that many factories in the garment, carpet, and sports equipment industries employ young children and subject workers to long hours, poor pay, physical and verbal abuse, and unhealthy working conditions. Some contend that consumers, businesses, governments, and labor unions should take direct action to curb such abuses by raising public awareness about child labor, banning imports of sweatshop-made products, or establishing humane workplace codes. Others, however, maintain that such actions would be too difficult to monitor. Furthermore, many developing nations argue that the anti-sweatshop campaign is simply an attempt to protect American industries from competition with cheaper third world imports.

Women who shop at upscale clothing stores have a connection with Nancy Peñaloza. She makes the clothes they wear to work. For the past nine years, the thirtyish seamstress has been sewing business suits that retail for $120 and up. Her cut: $6 per outfit. She is able to feed her family by putting in at least 56 hours a week, usually taking home $207. Unlike the women who wear her suits, Peñaloza gets no vacation or holidays off. And her employer does not pay her Social Security taxes.

"The shop is hot in the summer and cold in winter, and the boss is angry and screams," she says in halting English. "I cannot ask him questions because I am scared he will hit me. There is one bathroom for 100 people. If I were to ask for overtime pay, I would be fired."

Peñaloza's bleak account may conjure images of a Third World sweat-

Reprinted from Charles S. Clark, "Child Labor and Sweatshops: The Issues," *CQ Researcher*, August 16, 1996, by permission of the Congressional Quarterly, Inc.

shop, but as she revealed recently, she works in New York's famous garment district. She went public with her story in July 1996, appearing at the behest of the Labor Department before a conference of apparel industry executives, human rights activists and Labor officials, including then Secretary Robert B. Reich.

The return of sweatshops

Sweatshops and child labor—supposedly eradicated in the U.S. early in the twentieth century—have re-emerged dramatically on the global landscape, just as the twentieth century is wrapping up.

Since 1995, several events have propelled the issue onto American consumers' radar screens. In August 1995, law enforcement officers freed 72 illegal Thai immigrants who were being held behind barbed-wire in a compound in El Monte, Calif., near Los Angeles. They had been working as virtual slaves in an around-the-clock garment factory. During the trial of the owners, the workers said they had been paid 69 cents an hour to fill the racks of such American stores as Montgomery Ward's and Sears.[1]

In Canada in 1995, a 12-year-old boy drew world attention to the tragedy of child labor. Craig Kielburger, of Thornhill, Ont., founded the group Free the Children after hearing about the assassination of a Pakistani boy his own age who had been agitating against child labor. Craig gathered thousands of signatures calling for an import ban on products made with child labor and presented the petition to Canadian Prime Minister Jean Chretien.[2]

In May 1996, TV talk-show host Kathie Lee Gifford found herself being vilified after a human rights activist charged that her Wal-Mart fashion line was being produced with child and sweatshop labor. But Gifford surprised her critics. Newly sensitized to the problem of child labor, she re-emerged as an activist and weathered the unflattering publicity. "I want to leave this planet a very different place for my children," she told a congressional panel in July. "Why should other children be denied childhood—the basic right to bounce a ball, to play with jacks, to be safe? Why should my child be born to privilege and others to suffering?"[3]

Around the world, there are at least 73 million child laborers[4] ages 10-14, according to the United Nations' International Labour Organization (ILO) in Geneva, Switzerland. The ILO puts the figure for working children of all ages at up to 200 million, noting that 25 percent of all the children in Africa are working. In Asia the figure is 18 percent, in Latin America, 7 percent.

Most labor abuses take place in industries producing everyday products such as clothing, toys, sneakers, carpets and sports equipment. But some of the worst cruelties are found in areas where household slave labor is common, such as the Sudan, and in the underground world of forced child prostitution, which is rampant in Thailand and the Philippines.[5]

The dangers of child labor are not always apparent to the employers and parents who encourage it. "Pound for pound, children breathe more air, eat more food and drink more water than adults," says Philip J. Landrigan, a pediatrician at New York City's Mount Sinai Medical Center. "So if there are chemical contaminants in the workplace, children will be exposed to more of them. Children are also less biologically mature and less physically strong, which makes them more susceptible to injury. They're more likely to trip or get caught in machinery, and their bodies have more trouble breaking down chemical toxins and excreting them. Finally, children may be said to 'have a longer shelf-life,' which means that after exposure to, say, dangerous benzine or asbestos, they have more years ahead of them in which to develop diseases."

Experts say the child labor problem has worsened in recent years with the consolidation of the U.S. retail industry into a few huge conglomerates. These giants seek competitive advantages by "out-sourcing," or sub-contracting, to low-paying suppliers around the world. In 1987 the 20 biggest U.S. apparel companies accounted for 33 percent of domestic sales, according to the Census Bureau. By 1992, the share of the 20 largest had climbed to 41 percent of sales. Wal-Mart, K Mart and J.C. Penney, to name a few, have emerged as global empires that farm out thousands of manufacturing contracts.

Experts say the child labor problem has worsened in recent years with the consolidation of the U.S. retail industry into a few huge conglomerates.

The impact worldwide has been "growing insecurity and a downward spiral in labor standards," according to Neil Kearney, president of the International Textile, Garment and Leather Workers Union. "El Salvador, for example, has gained 50,000 jobs in the last 10 years, and its exports have jumped 4,000 percent. But its real wages have been halved. Its women can't afford to buy the clothes they make, and people who protest are subject to rape and murder."

Within the United States, analysts note, the garment industry's threats to send work overseas have brought down wages while easing the way for sweatshop operators to take advantage of frightened illegal immigrants desperate for work. A 1994 study by the General Accounting Office found that 2,000 of the 6,000 garment shops in New York City could be called sweatshops, and 4,500 out of 5,000 in Los Angeles. "You can have a sweatshop even if it's air-conditioned," says Jay Mazur, president of the Union of Needletrades, Industrial and Textile Employees (UNITE). "They violate wage and hour laws, pay no taxes, use child labor and require homework. In this New World Order of the global village, the laws haven't followed the changes."

Who is accountable for labor abuses?

Many companies agree that there is a problem, and in response many have created codes of conduct and supplier-monitoring programs. But others—including several California retailers who supposedly sold garments made in the El Monte sweatshop—say the abuses are not their fault because they have no control over their subcontractors. Overseas, they point out, suppliers must operate within the local cultures, economies and laws, where the American notion that children belong in school is often dismissed as quaint.

"In some Latin American and African countries, a child's right to schooling is related to birth order," notes an ILO study. "Older siblings receive preference for schooling, and parents are reported to be making large financial investments in older children in the expectation that they will . . . help finance the education of younger brothers and sisters" who are currently working.[6]

Finally, businesses point out that boycotts of sweatshop operators either by consumers or company managers can backfire. When the Pakistani carpet industry lost $10 million in orders because of a government crackdown on violators, the buyers simply went to neighboring India or Nepal, where child labor is also common.[7]

Changing the apparel industry will be difficult "because it's competitive, and people want a good price," says Jonathan Mudd, public policy manager for the Gap clothing chain, considered a leader in opposing worker exploitation. "But sweatshops and child labor are very topical now. People are talking about it in the carpool, not just in some ninth-floor office. A company can no longer ignore its social responsibility."

American consumers appear to be warming to such responsibility. A convincing 84 percent of adults surveyed recently would be willing to pay an extra $1 on a $20 garment if it were guaranteed not to have been made with sweatshop or child labor. And 66 percent said they would be more likely to patronize stores that cooperate with law enforcement to prevent sweatshops.[8]

But in today's global economy, it is difficult to make comforting distinctions between products fashioned according to America's usual standards of fair treatment and those turned out in the developing world, where child labor and sweatshops are built into local economies. Nor is it possible to know which American-made products reflect such standards.

"Forced labor is illegal in most parts of the world, and yet it is on the increase in Asia, Africa and Latin America because children are profitable and easily exploitable," says Rep. James P. Moran, D-Va., who closely follows the issue. "We as consumers are at fault. We want cheap handmade products without asking whose hands were on them."

As lawmakers and social activists work to curb labor exploitation, the following issues are being debated.

Government intervention

About 35 million soccer balls, or 80 percent of the world's annual supply, are produced in Pakistan. In the spring of 1995, members of Congress and the press alleged that children stitch as many as one-fourth of Pakistan's soccer balls, working 8–12 hours a day for as little as six cents an hour. Many of the children are bonded servants.

Pakistani employers scramble to hide children whenever human rights activists arrive to inspect conditions. Western journalists attempting to investigate have been threatened and assaulted.[9]

Like most countries, Pakistan has child-labor laws on the books, notably the 1991 Employment of Children Act. Pakistan's 1973 Constitution prohibits child labor, and the nation has ratified the 1989 United Nations Convention on the Rights of the Child. (Pakistan, however, is not among the 49 nations that have ratified the ILO's 1973 convention requiring a minimum working age of 15.)

As is often the case in the Third World, there is a yawning gap in Pakistan between law and reality. "The complicity of the state in the bonded labor system is explicitly illustrated by the fact that employers of bonded laborers are rarely arrested, prosecuted or punished for holding workers in bondage," says a Human Rights Watch study of Pakistan. "Furthermore, employers usually escape punishment for illegal confinement, rape or physical abuse of bonded laborers, all of which are clearly prohibited under the Pakistan Penal Code."[10]

In July 1996, Pakistani Labor Minister Ghulam Akbar Lasi announced that he had ordered local authorities to raid factories employing children. "They will conduct surprise visits to those areas where soccer balls are being made," he said. "If they find children working over there, they will arrest the contractors and report to me in a month," he said. The government says that, already, from January 1995 to March 1996, it has conducted 7,003 raids and prosecuted 2,538 employers, levying $1,428 fines and/or two to five years in prison.

Businesses point out that boycotts of sweatshop operators either by consumers or company managers can backfire.

Other Third World governments have made headlines by taking action. In India in 1995, then Prime Minister P.V. Narishma announced a plan to relieve 2 million children from work duties by the year 2000. Essentially, parents would receive monthly stipends and food rations in return for enrolling their children in school.

Meanwhile, many Indian industries, including hand-made carpet manufacturing, still use child labor, says newspaper reporter K. Arora, of *United News of India*. "Banning it is not practical because the carpets are made in rural villages, not in [more easily watched] cities," he says. "Today there is more awareness of child labor, and women's non-governmental organizations have protested it. But often the guy who writes about it or discusses it at the office water cooler is himself using it at home."

Uneven enforcement of the law in India has even drawn international lending institutions into the debate. Francoise Remington, founder of Forgotten Children in Arlington, Va., says the World Bank is financing major coal mining and dam construction projects in India that employ young children. She told a House subcommittee in July 1996 that since 1988 she has visited numerous factories in India and estimates there are 55 million Indian workers ages 6–14.[11]

Human rights advocates want the United States and European nations to ban all imports made by bonded labor. They demand that international lenders only aid businesses that comply with fair labor standards and that governments work out procedures for on-site inspections. They also want industrialized countries to suspend tariff benefits for offending countries. "Ultimately," writes consumer advocate Ralph Nader, "standing up to the cruelty of child labor will require the United States to challenge or quit the anti-democratic, anti-child" World Trade Organization (WTO).[12]

But to some observers, such aggressive actions run the risk of appearing to interfere in the affairs of sovereign nations. John Donaldson, external affairs officer of the World Bank, says: "We do not condone anything illegal in countries in which we have projects, and I am not aware of anything illegal. We do take reports seriously and investigate them, but if someone under 18 is working in a non-hazardous job that is legal in his country, then there is not much we can do. The World Bank works on alleviating poverty and promoting education, which help more than anything mandated to end child labor."

In fact, developing countries charge that industrialized countries use child labor and other similar issues as an excuse for protectionist efforts to shield domestic industries against cheap imports. At a June 1996 ILO conference in Washington in which child labor topped the agenda, representatives of Bangladesh, Indonesia, Pakistan and the Philippines objected to proposed solutions that were not "trade-neutral."

Many Western business groups agreed, speaking of a "need to respect local culture and customs." Abraham Katz, president of the New York City–based United States Council for International Business, warned that no one-solution-fits-all-problems approach can deal constructively with this complex issue. The organized employers community believes that this issue is best tackled through cooperation, example and sympathetic assistance on the ground rather than politically motivated coercion on the part of wealthy importing countries. . . . There are cases in which contracting companies, under the threat of action in importing countries, emptied their factories of children, who were put on the street with no recourse but to engage in prostitution, begging or at best work in far-less-favorable conditions."[13]

Former Labor Secretary Reich agrees that trade restraints risk making things worse for exploited workers and children. "The World Trade Organization and other nations are not with us on this," he says. Our power to get the facts out is limited overseas," he adds, which is one reason he concentrated his department's efforts on U.S. companies. "If we have embarrassed some members of industry, I'm sorry, but it may be necessary."

Human rights advocates want the United States and European nations to ban all imports made by bonded labor.

For three years, Reich presided over a "No Sweat" campaign within the United States. The crackdown involves surprise inspections (Reich himself popped in on New York City sweatshops), fining companies and conducting hearings and conferences with businesses and nongovernmental organizations to search for voluntary solutions. The conferences typically focus on enhancing enforcement and education efforts.

Thus far, Reich's campaign has persuaded nearly 50 U.S. firms to monitor subcontractors to prevent labor abuses and 20 major importers to consider tougher codes of conduct. The department publishes a list of "Trendsetters"—companies that are making progress on curbing sweatshops and child labor—ranging from Abercrombie & Fitch to Victoria's Secret. The campaign has distributed 50 million information sheets dubbed "Clues for Consumers," and Reich is exploring a campaign to put "No Sweat" labels on international products.

Activists against labor abuse say Reich is doing yeoman's work. "Before the Department of Labor stepped in, this wasn't even recognized as an international problem," says UNITE's Mazur.

Developing countries charge that industrialized countries use child labor . . . as an excuse for protectionist efforts to shield domestic industries against cheap imports.

The Trendsetters list, which requires continuing efforts by companies for inclusion, has raised awareness in the industry, says the Gap's Mudd. "But the list could be a lot longer. Many of the smaller companies that are making progress are not getting recognized in the press in the way the Gap and Wal-Mart are."

Duncan Muir, a spokesman for Dallas-based J.C. Penney, complains that his firm did not make the list. "We encourage monitors, but we only require it if a supplier has previously violated the law," he says. "We have 6,600 suppliers in 80 countries, so it would be burdensome."

Peter J. Eide, manager of labor law policy at the U.S. Chamber of Commerce, questions the whole premise of Reich's campaign. "He has the Fair Labor Standards Act, so let him enforce it instead of talking about boycotts and shame," he says. "Now we've got the government saying which is a good company and which is a bad one. It's wholly inappropriate."

An opinion poll released in June 1996 by the International Mass Retail Association showed that 46 percent of Americans think that the U.S. and foreign governments have the main responsibility to police exploitive labor practices abroad, while only 29 percent said manufacturers are responsible, and 18 percent put the onus on retailers.

But companies that want the Labor Department to beef up its enforcement "have not been heard calling for increased funding for inspections," says Alan Howard, assistant to the president of UNITE. "That subjects the companies to fairly credible accusations of hypocrisy."

The responsibility of business

As Reich is wont to point out, the Labor Department employs only 800 inspectors to monitor compliance with wage and hour laws at 6.5 million U.S. worksites employing 110 million workers. If sweatshops and child labor are to be policed, he says, industry's active cooperation is essential.

Since the sweatshop issue has become front-page news—particularly after the Kathie Lee affair—many large retailers such as Wal-Mart and K Mart have announced new codes of conduct for subcontractors, beefed-up internal monitoring and plans to sever ties with suppliers who violate the rules.

In November 1995, the National Retail Federation, the largest industry group, established an "honor roll" of businesses that sign its new statement of principles, which has attracted 200 companies. The federation has developed a supplier non-compliance form" intended for use by the Labor Department to notify retailers of subcontractors who abuse the law.

The Sporting Goods Manufacturers Association lept into action following the soccer ball controversy. "The U.S. soccer industry has taken unprecedented steps to address the issue of child labor in a conscientious and responsible manner," Thomas J. Cove, the group's vice president, told the Labor Department in June 1996. "Representatives of several companies traveled to [Pakistan] accompanied by industry critics who assisted in their inquiry. At the same time, the industry . . . established a task force on global manufacturing practices to organize research and develop recommendations for joint action."

Despite such industry action, Cove argues that the news media has sensationalized some of the problems. He points to two surveys by human rights groups within Pakistan that found that the vast majority of soccer balls are stitched by workers over age 14. What's more, over half of the working children who reportedly do stitch an estimated 10–25 percent of Pakistan's soccer balls perform the work in their own homes. "The soccer industry does not seek out child labor or compensate child stitchers differently than their adult counterparts," he said.

Others point to a more tepid performance by corporate America. "Companies differ in their degree of seriousness," says Pharis Harvey, executive director of the International Labor Rights Fund in Washington. "Over the past several months, more companies have realized that this is not an issue they can shrug off by saying, 'We have thousands of suppliers and don't know who they are so we're not responsible.' This was their common reaction a few years ago. Now, those with a great deal of equity value in their corporate name are the first to take steps because their products are traceable back to a company in the way that, say, Liz Claiborne is linked to Liz Claiborne Inc."

Nike founder Philip H. Knight [pays] workers in Indonesia about $2.20 a day while his own stock in Nike is worth $4.5 billion.

Two of the pioneers in corporate activism against sweatshops are Guess jeans and Levi Strauss. At Guess, says former General Counsel Stan Levy, quality-control inspectors are trained in the nuances of labor law so that compliance monitoring is "integrated into the production process every step of the way."

Levi Strauss, credited with inaugurating the first such integrated approach in 1991, has set an example for the industry by dropping suppliers in Myanmar, China and the Pacific island of Saipan who had violated labor laws. "It's innately how we do things, part of how we measure performance," says Senior Vice President John Ermatinger. "It's not as an add-on or a burden." Levi Strauss has also simplified monitoring by reducing its number of suppliers.

According to Howard of UNITE, the company that has come farthest is the Gap. "They're in a class by themselves, not because they've accomplished so much, but because they've really gone out there in setting up the first truly independent monitoring operation," he says.

In December 1995, following charges that its clothing suppliers in El Salvador ran sweatshops, GAP representatives met with three American activist groups: the National Labor Committee, Business for Social Responsibility and the Interfaith Center for Corporate Responsibility. They announced formation of the Independent Monitoring Group of El Salvador, which by March 1996 had reached agreement with Salvadoran managers, workers and union leaders to strive toward a "humane, productive, successful business." As a pilot program, the Gap hired two full-time compliance officers to enforce its newly updated Code of Vendor Conduct, which specifies worldwide safety and sanitation standards, as well as limits on management prerogatives, in factories and worker dormitories.

Mudd views many other corporate codes as too subject to interpretation, resulting in confusion as workers look for their rights and responsibilities while managers strive to satisfy their clients. "Ours is a living document," he says. While he is hopeful about the monitoring experiment, the fact that the Gap pays the compliance officers invites skepticism about their independence, he says. "They are open to claims of being co-opted, but they have to get their money from somewhere. Hopefully, they should be like the Maytag repairman—not very busy but ready to swing into action."

Walt Disney and Nike

One of the least responsive companies, according to Howard, is Walt Disney, which markets children's clothing bearing images from hit movies such as "The Hunchback of Notre Dame" and "The Lion King." But the billion-dollar-a-year business depends, Disney's critics allege, on workers in Haiti who make 28 cents an hour.

The National Labor Committee, the union group that confronted Kathie Lee Gifford, has produced a muckraking video called "Mickey Mouse Goes to Haiti." To the familiar Disney tune "Hi ho, hi ho, it's off to work we go," the video reveals shocking footage of shantytowns where Haiti's garment workers toil. The workers reportedly earn five cents for every $11.99 children's outfit they produce. "They treat us badly, like we are dirt, like we were dumb, with no respect," a worker says. "You can't even speak to the bosses. If you try, they fire you. The supervisors are always screaming at us to work faster. The pressure to make the quota is great."

Thomas Deegan, Disney's vice president for corporate communications, says that Disney subcontractors "follow all applicable employment and environmental laws." He says the company inspects factories with which it has direct supplier contracts, and that "inspections to guarantee product quality have been augmented with additional checks into workplace safety and legal compliance."

In checking out the charges, Disney says it consulted the U.S. ambassador to Haiti, Washington human rights monitors, two Disney licensees in Haiti and a business group. The company also sent a representative to Haiti. "Having thoroughly investigated these matters, we have been able to find no evidence of minimum wage, child labor or other violations in the manufacture of Disney merchandise," Deegan says. "We believe that our licensees are managing their manufacturing operations in a reasonable manner."

Howard argues that "obeying the laws is just the beginning of a corporation's responsibility. In a world from which they earn enormous profits, they have a responsibility to put resources back in," he says.

The owners of the factories used by Disney point out that they're running a business, not a charity. "All we have to sell is our cheap labor," said one. "Our workers are weak and anemic and produce only 60 percent of what workers sew in the U.S.," said another.[14]

Nike spokeswoman Donna Gibbs argues that the average wage of a Nike worker in Indonesia is double the local minimum wage.

Also in the human rights hot seat has been the highly successful Nike athletic shoe company. It is regularly attacked as an exploiter of Asian labor by Jeffrey Ballinger, who runs the organization Press for Change, and by *New York Times* columnist Bob Herbert. In June 1996 Herbert slam-dunked Nike founder Philip H. Knight for paying workers in Indonesia about $2.20 a day while his own stock in Nike is worth $4.5 billion. "More than a third of Nike's products are manufactured in Indonesia, a human rights backwater where the minimum wage was deliberately set below the subsistence level in order to attract foreign investment," Herbert writes. "What's next, employees who'll work for a bowl of gruel?"[15]

Nike spokeswoman Donna Gibbs argues that the average wage of a Nike worker in Indonesia is double the local minimum wage, that the company offers them free meals and health care, and that the company has monitors in 25 countries. "Could there be abuses? There could be," she says. "It's better to have companies like Nike with a brand image at stake operating in these countries to assure that abuses don't occur."[16]

Overall, says Robert Dunn, president of Business for Social Responsibility, "the good news is that over the last few years there has been a concentrated effort by business leaders to get their arms around the problem. They're still experimenting, but companies are making a clear commitment. They are aligning themselves with partners who recognize the problem throughout their supply chain. It's an enormous and complex problem that has raged for centuries in some countries. They are looking to find collective solutions and stop pointing fingers."

Notes

1. Seven members of the Thai family that ran the El Monte sweatshop pleaded guilty to involuntary slavery charges and were sentenced to prison terms ranging from two to seven years. In addition, U.S. District Judge Audrey B. Collins ordered the family to pay $4.5 million to the workers, one of whom was kept imprisoned for seven years.

2. *Maclean's*, Dec. 11, 1995, p. 29. Craig Kielburger was inspired by the death of Iqbal Masih, a former child laborer who had received the 1994

Reebok Youth in Action award for his efforts against child labor.

3. Testimony before House International Relations Subcommittee on International Operations and Human Rights, July 15, 1996.

4. Millions of children work as bonded laborers, defined by the ILO as forced labor in payment for the debts of the child's parents or work offered under a false pretext form which children are not allowed to leave. Bonded child labor also includes children who are kidnapped and exported as prostitutes or camel riders, "recruited" for work on plantations and those maimed by criminal gangs and forced into beggary or other rackets.

5. For background, see "Prostitution," *The CQ Researcher,* June 11, 1993, pp. 505–528.

6. Assefa Bequele and Jo Boyden, eds., *Combating Child Labor* (1988), p. 7.

7. *The Economist,* June 3, 1995, p. 58.

8. The November 1995 survey was conducted by the Center for Ethical Concerns and the Department of Fashion Design and Merchandising at Marymount University in Arlington, Va.

9. Sydney Schanberg, *Life,* June 1, 1996, p. 38.

10. Human Rights Watch/Asia, "Contemporary Forms of Slavery in Pakistan," July 1995, p. 68.

11. Testimony before Subcommittee on International Operations and Human Rights, July 15, 1996.

12. Guest editorial in *USA Today,* June 21, 1996. For more on the WTO, see "Rethinking NAFTA," *The CQ Researcher,* June 7, 1996, pp. 481–504.

13. Testimony at International Labour Organization hearing at the Labor Department, June 28, 1996.

14. Quoted in Barry Berak, "Stitching Together a Crusade," *Los Angeles Times,* July 25, 1996.

15. *The New York Times,* June 10, 1996.

16. Quoted in *USA Today,* June 6, 1996.

An Indictment
of Sweatshops

Olivia Given

Olivia Given recently graduated from the University of Chicago with a bachelor's degree in psychology. She is an organizing committee member of the Youth Section of the Democratic Socialists of America.

Economic globalization—the expansion of corporate power to multinational domains—has led to the reemergence of sweatshops in the latter twentieth century. Many garment-industry companies boost their own profits by using manufacturers that discourage collective bargaining, pay low wages, and offer little or no employee benefits. These manufacturers typically prefer to hire young, uneducated women who work long hours to support their families. Sweatshop workers face myriad abuses, including verbal abuse, sexual harassment, physical punishment, and forced overtime. Because corporations are more interested in increasing profits than in ensuring workers' rights, anti-sweatshop measures have largely not been effective at curbing the exploitation of workers.

*W*hat is a sweatshop? The Department of Labor defines a work place as a sweatshop if it violates two or more of the most basic labor laws including child labor, minimum wage, overtime and fire safety laws. For many, the word sweatshop conjures up images of dirty, cramped, turn of the century New York tenements where immigrant women worked as seamstresses. High-rise tenement sweatshops still do exist, but, today, even large, brightly-lit factories can be the sites of rampant labor abuses.

Sweatshop workers report horrible working conditions including sub-minimum wages, no benefits, non-payment of wages, forced overtime, sexual harassment, verbal abuse, corporal punishment, and illegal firings. Children can often be found working in sweatshops instead of going to school. Sweatshop operators are notorious for avoiding giving maternity leave by firing pregnant women and forcing women workers to take birth control or to abort their pregnancies.

Sweatshop operators can best control a pool of workers that are igno-

Reprinted from Olivia Given, "Frequently Asked Questions About Sweatshops and Women Workers," at www.feminist.org/other/sweatfaq.html, September 1997, by permission of the author.

rant of their rights as workers. Therefore, bosses often refuse to hire unionized workers and intimidate or fire any worker suspected of speaking with union representatives or trying to organize her fellow workers.

I thought sweatshops were a thing of the past. Why are we hearing so much about them again? The notorious sweatshops of the age of Big Business (the late 19th and early 20th centuries) virtually disappeared after World War II because of increased government regulation of monopolies and the rise of trade unions. Sweatshops began to reappear again, however, during the 1980's and 1990's because of economic globalization. Today's economy is described as global because advancements in technology have made it possible for large corporations that were once confined to a specific geographic location to become large "multi-nationals."

The popularity of the "free" market following the fall of Communism and a rise in anti-union sentiment, coupled with government programs (like the North American Free Trade Agreement and the General Agreement on Tariffs and Trade) designed to encourage free trade, have hastened the globalization process. Large corporations are now free to seek out low-wage havens: impoverished countries where corporations benefit from oppressive dictatorial regimes that actively suppress workers' freedoms of speech and association. Even in North America, where the North American Free Trade Agreement (NAFTA) is supposed to enforce a minimum standard for workers' rights, corporations concentrate in maquiladoras, "free trade zones" that were created by NAFTA, where the workers' rights provisions of the Agreement simply do not apply.

Corporations have been fleeing countries with relatively prosperous economies and stable democracies in droves not only to take advantage of cheap labor, but to escape government scrutiny and criticism from human rights and workers' rights organizations. Guess? Clothing Co., for example, has always produced the majority of its goods in the U.S. but threatened to move 75% of this manufacturing to Mexico in 1996 in response to Department of Labor citations and highly publicized humanitarian campaigns about Guess?'s California contract sweatshops.

Sweatshops are nearly everywhere

Are there sweatshops in the U.S.? According to the Department of Labor, over 50% of U.S. garment factories are sweatshops. Many sweatshops are run in this country's apparel centers: California, New York, Dallas, Miami and Atlanta.

Where are most sweatshops? There are probably sweatshops in every country in the world—anywhere where there is a pool of desperate, exploitable workers. Logically, the poorer a country is the more exploitable its people are. Labor violations are, therefore, especially widespread in third world countries. Nike has been criticized for unethical labor practices in its Chinese, Vietnamese and Indonesian shoe factories, and Haitian garment factories have similarly been criticized. Non-profit groups have documented the labor violations of retailers like Phillips-Van · Heusen and the Gap in factories throughout Latin America.

As mentioned above, however, developing countries are not the only ones with sweatshops. Guess? Clothing Corporation, for example, has been cited numerous times by the Department of Labor for the use of contract sweatshops in California.

Who is a typical sweatshop worker? In the garment industry, the typical sweatshop worker is a woman (90% of all sweatshop workers are women). She is young and, often, missing the chance for an education because she must work long hours to support a family. In America, she is often a recent or undocumented immigrant. She is almost always non-union and usually unaware that, even if she is in this country illegally, she still has rights as a worker.

Sweatshop workers report horrible working conditions including sub-minimum wages, no benefits, non-payment of wages, forced overtime, sexual harassment, verbal abuse, corporal punishment, and illegal firings.

Which companies are operating sweatshops? Many of the companies directly running sweatshops are small and don't have much name recognition. However, virtually every retailer in the U.S. has ties to sweatshops. The U.S. is the biggest market for the garment industry and almost all the garment sales in this country are controlled by 5 corporations: Wal-Mart, JC Penney, Sears, The May Company (owns and operates Lord & Taylor, Hecht's, Filene's and others) and Federated Department Stores (owns and operates Bloomingdale's, Macy's, Burdine's, Stern's and others).

Several industry leaders have been cited for labor abuses by the Department of Labor. Of these Guess? Clothing Co. is one of the worst offenders—Guess? was suspended indefinitely from the Department of Labor's list of "good guys" because their contractors were cited for so many sweatshop violations.

Other companies contract out their production to overseas manufacturers whose labor rights violations have been exposed by U.S. and international human rights groups. These include Nike, Disney, Wal-Mart, Reebok, Phillips-Van Heusen, the Gap, Liz Claiborne and Ralph Lauren.

Don't these company officials feel guilty for using sweatshops? Large corporations almost always use contract manufacturing firms to produce their goods. In this way, corporations separate themselves from the production of their own goods and try to claim that the working conditions under which their goods are produced are not their responsibility.

In fact, it is the corporations that dictate the conditions of their workers. Corporations squeeze their contractors into paying sub-minimum wages. Large retailers and retail chains pressure contract manufacturers by refusing to pay more that a rock-bottom price for manufacturing orders. They also demand that their manufacturing contractors guarantee them a profit by buying back unsold merchandise at the end of each season. Manufacturers deal with this financial squeeze not by cutting their own profits, but by cutting workers' wages and benefits, and by compromising workers' physical safety.

Many corporations also refuse to contract to union shops. So, even if a contractor does want to pay their workers a reasonable wage and allow them their freedom of association, he/she will probably be run out of business. In the end, it is the workers who pay for corporate greed.

How do American companies get away with running sweatshops? Unfortunately the Department of Labor does not have enough personnel to inspect every workplace for labor violations. The Department of Labor only requires companies to have an *internal* monitoring policy, as opposed to an external monitoring policy where site inspections and evaluations would be unannounced and conducted by impartial parties. With internal monitoring there is no way to know whether companies are telling the truth about the conditions in their own factories. Many companies, like Nike, pay private accounting firms to come into their factories and assess the working conditions as "independent" monitors.

Even when companies are caught violating workers' rights, the punishment is often nominal. Fines that may seem hefty to us are insignificant to companies reaping multi-million dollar profits.

Why do foreign governments let foreign companies come into their country and exploit their people? The truth is, business and government are a lot more connected to each other than most people think. Our economy rewards the highest bidder among consumers and the lowest bidder among producers. Foreign governments, desperate for economic gain, often deliberately set their national minimum wage below what it would actually take a worker to support herself and her family. The citizens of a country starve and suffer while the elite class and corrupt government officials reap the benefits of globalization.

Responses to sweatshop exploitation

What is the U.S. government doing about sweatshops? The Fair Labor Standards Act of 1938 officially prohibits sweatshops. However, because of understaffing at the Department of Labor and corporations' strategies for distancing themselves from the production of their goods by contracting production out to many different manufacturers, enforcement is lax. In 1997 Stop Sweatshops Bills were introduced in Congress that would amend the Fair Labor Standards Act to hold companies responsible for the labor violations of their contractors.

President Clinton has also created an Apparel Industry Task Force of both labor rights and corporate interests to address the issue of sweatshops. The Task Force's first resolution, however, failed to address many important issues for workers. The Task Force does not require member-corporations to pay their workers a living wage, instead requiring only the, often substandard, minimum wage set by the government of a corporation's host country. The resolution allows member-corporations to force their workers to labor as many as 60 hours a week during regular business circumstances, and even more under vaguely defined "extraordinary" business circumstances. The Task Force is due to release its second report in November 1997. However, reports indicate that corporate interests continue to be unyielding to the requests of human and workers' rights groups.

Can the U.S. government enforce U.S. labor laws on U.S. companies operating abroad? No, it can't. This is precisely the reason that many U.S. companies move their production operations overseas. Multi-national corporations *actively seek out* markets where wages are low, unions are outlawed and desperate people will work for almost any price. Nike, for example, first moved production out of the U.S. to Taiwan and South Korea when American workers organized to demand a reasonable wage. Then, when democracy took hold in Taiwan and South Korea, Nike moved production again, this time to China, Indonesia and Vietnam, all countries run by dictatorial military regimes that violently suppress workers' rights.

Multi-national corporations actively seek out *markets where wages are low, unions are outlawed and desperate people will work for almost any price.*

What are relations like between the U.S. government and the governments of countries where U.S. businesses are operating sweatshops? Ironically, the U.S. gives humanitarian and other types of aid to countries whose poverty is, in part, a result of unscrupulous U.S. business operations. The U.S. government gives lip-service to workers' and human rights while promoting the business climates most conducive to sweatshops, namely, through NAFTA and the U.S.'s "laissez-faire" attitude towards the growing markets in East and Southeast Asia.

What is the alternative to a sweatshop? Corporations set up sweatshops in the name of "competition". In reality these corporations are not facing profit losses or bankruptcy, just too little profit! During the twentieth century, workers real wages have gone down while CEOs' salaries have skyrocketed. In 1965 the average CEO made 44 times the average factory worker. Today, the average CEO makes 212 times the salary of the average worker.

Corporations have skewed priorities. Many are putting expenses like CEO salaries and advertising costs before the well-being of their workers. For example, a Haitian worker sewing children's pajamas for Disney would have to toil full-time for 14.5 years to earn what Michael Eisner makes in one hour! Here's another staggering statistic: Nike could pay all its individual workers enough to feed and clothe themselves and their families if it would just devote 1% of its advertising budget to workers' salaries each year! Corporations falsely claim that they are victims of the global economy when, in fact, corporations help create and maintain this system.

3

A Defense of Sweatshops

Murray Weidenbaum

Murray Weidenbaum is chairman of the Center for the Study of American Business at Washington University in St. Louis, Missouri.

American buyers should not force overseas sweatshops to abide by a seemingly more enlightened labor standard that would guarantee factory workers good pay and shorter hours. Such a requirement would force many overseas manufacturers out of business; in addition, U.S. companies would face increased price competition from foreign industries who would continue to use sweatshop labor. Instead of requiring sweatshops to adopt higher labor standards, consumers should recognize that the use of child labor and low-wage workers is a normal stage in the industrial development of poor nations. As these nations become more economically successful, they will abandon exploitative labor practices.

E conomists seem destined to speak out in favor of unpopular causes. A current case in point is the effort to force U.S. companies to promise not to buy merchandise produced overseas under "sweatshop" conditions. Unfortunately, that is a misguided effort whose results are likely to be counterproductive.

I am not defending companies who engage in illegal labor practices, at home or abroad. The law should be fully obeyed and U.S. firms have a very good record on that score. Lawbreaking is not what the debate on "sweatshop" labor is all about. The basic concern is that, by our enlightened standards, many of those foreign workers are poorly paid and poorly treated—and too young, as well.

New labor standards would be disastrous

Supposedly, if American buyers would force their foreign suppliers to pay their workers more and work them shorter hours, that would set a new and better labor standard for those backwoods countries. Sounds good? In practice, that would be a disaster for all concerned.

Local firms not selling to idealistic U.S. buyers would be hard pressed to keep their workers. If they matched those new wage scales, they would

Reprinted from Murray Weidenbaum, "In Defense of Sweatshops," *Investor's Business Daily*, February 11, 1997, by permission of the author and Scoop Media.

lose their customers. Cries of Yankee imperialism would quickly be heard.

But that situation would not last long. High-paying American firms would soon find that competitors in other developed nations—not inhibited by our idealism—would be producing at lower cost and undercut our firms in markets all over the world.

Yet the concern over low-paid workers merits a positive response. After all, the United States started off as a poor country, with a substantial work force of child labor and low-paid adult workers, too. We did not overcome that situation because the then more industrialized nations in Europe pressured us to change our ways.

Rather, as our economy progressed, families now earning higher incomes could afford to keep their children in school longer. Whether intentionally or not, the current-day protectionists would delay the development of the poorer economies and thus deter their adoption of more enlightened labor policies. (By the way, we still use prison labor, and defense contractors are required to make some purchases from the Federal Prison Industries.)

We should not forget the alternative facing the employees of the so-called "sweatshop" contractors. Often, it is unemployment or criminal activity (child prostitution is widespread in some developing nations). For many, work in a factory, albeit way below U.S. standards, is a far better choice.

Whether intentionally or not, the current-day protectionists would delay the development of the poorer economies and thus deter their adoption of more enlightened labor policies.

On a more positive note, we can consider the examples of national economies which, as they grew, abandoned "sweatshop practices." Early in the twentieth century, Japan moved from poverty to wealth, as did South Korea in the last half of the twentieth century. Right now, nations in Southeast Asia are undergoing a similar transformation. In each of these cases, rising portions of the population advanced to better paying jobs—not as the result of idealism but from changing economic circumstances.

We should not overlook the interests of our own workers. The ingredients for better jobs and rising living standards are well known—education, training, applying science and technology to develop new products, and new opportunities for entrepreneurship.

It is understandable that American-based unions are in the forefront of the opposition to low-cost "sweatshops" overseas. The distaste for competition is universal. After all, many business firms who pay large amounts of lip service to the notion of free markets push for government policies to inhibit their competitors. Their attachment to the beauty of the competitive marketplace focuses on the merits of competition among their suppliers. As we discount the self-serving arguments of some businesses, we should be equally alert to the special-interest claims of labor organizations.

Moreover, it is appropriate to recall the point made so clearly by No-bel Laureate Milton Friedman in an earlier disputation: If his parents were not willing to work so long and hard under "sweatshop" conditions, they could not have earned the money to invest in his education. We should all be grateful for that investment by a previous generation of Fried-mans—and many others like them—and for the circumstances that en-abled them to make that enlightened choice.

4

Sweatshops Must Be Recognized as a Human Rights Violation

Timothy Ryan

*Timothy Ryan is a representative in South Asia for the American Feder-
ation of Labor–Congress of Industrial Organizations (AFL-CIO).*

The life and death of Iqbal Masih, a Pakistani child activist, reveals
that sweatshops are not solely the result of economic hardship. After escaping from a six-year bondage as a carpet weaver, Masih
campaigned against the exploitation of child laborers in industrial
plants before his murder at the age of twelve. Like most child laborers and bonded workers, Masih was a member of a religious minority. This fact proves that racial, religious, and ethnic discrimination play a large role in the proliferation of sweatshops. The
exploitation of poor workers in developing countries must, therefore, be seen as a human rights violation and not purely as a con-
sequence of poverty.

Anyone who knew Iqbal Masih, the 12-year-old boy assassinated in
1995 in Lahore, Pakistan, by someone believed to be a feudal landlord
and carpet manufacturer, was struck by his brilliance.

I don't simply mean his intellectual abilities, though once rescued
from slavery at a carpet loom this young activist demonstrated a tremendous aptitude for learning. He went through five years of school curricu-
lum in three. Although malnutrition and abuse left him, at the age of 12,
physically smaller and more frail than my nine-year-old daughter, it was
clear that his mind, his ambition, and his spirit burned brightly.

When I saw him in December 1994 in Karachi on his return from the
United States, where he received a Reebok Human Rights Award, he was
filled with the excitement of his first airplane ride, a new Instamatic camera, his visit with other schoolchildren in Boston, and the unimaginable
promise that one day he might attend a university. Brandeis University
had pledged to give a four-year scholarship to Iqbal when he finished his

Reprinted from Timothy Ryan, "Iqbal Masih's Life: A Call to Human Rights Vigilance," *The
Christian Science Monitor*, May 3, 1995, by permission of the author.

studies in Pakistan.

Then someone motivated by greed, by fear, by hatred, pulled the trigger of a shotgun and obliterated this promise.

Iqbal's courage

I first met Iqbal in 1994 through my work with the Bonded Labor Liberation Front (BLLF) as a representative of the American Federation of Labor–Congress of Industrial Organizations (AFL-CIO) in South Asia.

The BLLF has worked dauntlessly for years to free thousands of bonded and child laborers, Iqbal among them. After working six years at a carpet loom, starting at the age of four, Iqbal was rescued by the BLLF when he was 10.

Iqbal's rescue was due in no small part to his own guts. In December 1994 he told me that one day two years beforehand, in the village where he was enslaved as a carpet weaver, he saw BLLF posters declaring that bonded and child labor was illegal under Pakistan law and secretly contacted BLLF activists. At the risk of his own life, Iqbal led the BLLF to the carpet looms where they rescued hundreds of children, who might still be in slavery if not for his courage.

It seems medieval, and perhaps it is, but for years carpet manufacturers, brick kiln owners, landowners, and manufacturers of sporting goods and other products in Pakistan have maintained an unrelenting grip on bonded laborers and children. Some estimates run as high as 20 million bonded and child laborers. At least half a million children are employed in the carpet trade alone.

Because of the current tension between Islamic and Christian communities in Pakistan, some apologists want to paint the killing of Iqbal as a purely religious matter. On one level this is a mere smoke screen. But on a more complex and sinister level, there is some connection between the fact that Iqbal was Christian and the fact that he was pressed into slavery in the first place.

Iqbal's story has an economic and political subtext: Politicians and businessmen in Pakistan form a tight web of relationships based on kin, clan, and caste. They count on family members who occupy positions of authority in local, provincial, national, and police bodies to look the other way when laws are violated, or, in many cases, to actively participate in crimes against workers and minorities.

The problem is not solely economic

Poverty is often the surface excuse for a problem that has deeper roots. It's a fallacy to see Iqbal's death solely as the result of brutal economics, rather than the outcome of broader, more pervasive violations of fundamental human rights.

On one level Iqbal's story is surely economic—poor people have less education, less income, less power than the rich. Even though it was outlawed in 1992 under Pakistan's Bonded Labor Abolition Act, the "advance" system that bonds people to their employers continues unabated. This system ensnared Iqbal at the age of four. The BLLF has taken some cases to court, but police and employer intimidation, along with judges' unwillingness to enforce the law, has prevented any prosecutions under the 1992 law.

It's at a deeper, generally hidden level that Iqbal's tragedy intersects with millions of Pakistani citizens and helps to explain the oppressive social and cultural patterns that are partly responsible for his death.

The fact is, most people who are bonded and enslaved are converted Muslims, indigenous tribal people, Hindus, and Christians—in short, anyone outside the mainstream of Sunni Islamic society. This insight reveals the intrinsic link between "economic" or "labor" issues and pervasive problems of intolerance and discrimination based on race, language, and ethnicity.

It's a fallacy to see Iqbal's death solely as the result of brutal economics, rather than the outcome of broader, more pervasive violations of fundamental human rights.

So we're not just talking here about poverty and economic hardship, or one brave little boy's death. We're talking about enslavement based on race and language and religion, about the treatment of human beings as commodities, as slave labor, and the slow grinding to death of people who not only are denied economic advancement, but also a chance at education, decent housing, clean water—the things that make life livable.

Iqbal's death must have a greater meaning beyond the tragedy of a bright meteor snuffed out by greed and corruption. His experience implores us to look beyond "poverty" or "economic hardship" as an explanation of why so many men, women, and children in traditional societies are exploited—to see the rights of child workers and bonded workers as part of a continuum of overall human rights that must be defended at all costs.

5

Sweatshops Often Benefit the Economies of Developing Nations

Allen R. Myerson

Allen R. Myerson is a writer for the New York Times.

The economies of third world nations often benefit from the introduction of low-wage manufacturing jobs. Many economists maintain that these "sweatshop" jobs can offer the world's poor a release from malnourishment and destitution. The recent economic development of several nations—including Japan, South Korea, and Taiwan—is rooted in the proliferation of industrial plants that utilize cheap labor. Typically, the alternatives to such jobs are unemployment, increased poverty, or work in even more abusive, hazardous environments. Those concerned about the exploitation of workers must recognize that the presence of sweatshops in the developing world is actually the first step toward economic prosperity.

For more than a century, accounts of sweatshops have provoked outrage. From the works of Charles Dickens and Lincoln Steffens to today's television reports, the image of workers hunched over their machines for meager rewards has been a banner of reform.

In 1996, companies like Nike and Wal-Mart and celebrities like Kathie Lee Gifford struggled to defend themselves after reports of the torturous hours and low pay of the workers who produce their upscale footwear or downmarket fashions. Anxious corporate spokesmen sought to explain the plants as a step up for workers in poor countries. A weeping Mrs. Gifford denied knowing about the conditions.

Now some of the nation's leading economists, with solid liberal and academic credentials, are offering a much broader, more principled rationale. Economists like Jeffrey D. Sachs of Harvard and Paul Krugman of the Massachusetts Institute of Technology say that low-wage plants making clothing and shoes for foreign markets are an essential first step toward modern prosperity in developing countries.

Mr. Sachs, a leading adviser and shock therapist to nations like Bolivia, Russia and Poland, is now working on the toughest cases of all, the economies of sub-Saharan Africa. He is just back from Malawi, where malaria afflicts almost all its 13 million people and AIDS affects 1 in 10; the lake that provided much of the country's nourishment is fished out.

When asked during a Harvard panel discussion whether there were too many sweatshops in such places, Mr. Sachs answered facetiously. "My concern is not that there are too many sweatshops but that there are too few," he said.

Mr. Sachs, who has visited low-wage factories around the world, is opposed to child or prisoner labor and other outright abuses. But many nations, he says, have no better hope than plants paying mere subsistence wages. "Those are precisely the jobs that were the steppingstone for Singapore and Hong Kong," he said, "and those are the jobs that have to come to Africa to get them out of their backbreaking rural poverty."

Rising stakes

The stakes in the battle over sweatshops are high and rising. Clinton Administration officials say commerce with the major developing nations like China, Indonesia and Mexico is crucial for America's own continued prosperity. Corporate America's manufacturing investments in developing nations more than tripled in 15 years to $56 billion in 1995—not including the vast numbers of plants there that contract with American companies.

In matters of trade and commerce, economists like Mr. Sachs, who has also worked with several government agencies, are influential. A consensus among economists helped persuade President Bill Clinton, who had campaigned against President George Bush's plan of lowered restrictions, to ram global and North American trade pacts through Congress.

Paradoxically, economists' support of sweatshops represents a sort of optimism. Until the mid-1980's, few thought that third world nations could graduate to first world status in a lifetime, if ever. "When I went to graduate school in the early to mid-1970's," Mr. Krugman said, "it looked like being a developed country was really a closed club." Only Japan had made a convincing jump within the past century.

Low-wage plants making clothing and shoes for foreign markets are an essential first step toward modern prosperity in developing countries.

Those economists who believed that developing nations could advance often prescribed self-reliance and socialism, warning against foreign investment as a form of imperialism. Advanced nations invested in the developing world largely to extract oil, coffee, bananas and other resources but created few new jobs or industries. Developing nations, trying to lessen their reliance on manufactured imports, tried to bolster domestic industries for the home market. But these protected businesses were often inefficient and the local markets too small to sustain them.

From wigs to cars

Then the Four Tigers— Hong Kong, Singapore, South Korea and Taiwan— began to roar. They made apparel, toys, shoes and, at least in South Korea's case, wigs and false teeth, mostly for export. Within a generation, their national incomes climbed from about 10 percent to 40 percent of American incomes. Singapore welcomed foreign plant owners while South Korea shunned them, building industrial conglomerates of its own. But the first stage of development had one constant. "It's always sweatshops," Mr. Krugman said

These same nations now export cars and computers, and the economists have revised their views of sweatshops. "The overwhelming mainstream view among economists is that the growth of this kind of employment is tremendous good news for the world's poor," Mr. Krugman said.

Unlike the corporate apologists, economists make no attempt to prettify the sweatshop picture. Mr. Krugman, who writes a column for *Slate* magazine called "The Dismal Scientist," describes sweatshop owners as "soulless multinationals and rapacious local entrepreneurs, whose only concern was to take advantage of the profit opportunities offered by cheap labor." But even in a nation as corrupt as Indonesia, he says, industrialization has reduced the portion of malnourished children from more than half in 1975 to a third today.

"The growth of [sweatshop] employment is tremendous good news for the world's poor," [Paul] Krugman said.

In judging the issue of child labor also, Mr. Krugman is a pragmatist, asking what else is available. It often isn't education. In India, for example, destitute parents sometimes sell their children to Persian Gulf begging syndicates whose bosses mutilate them for a higher take, he says. "If that is the alternative, it is not so easy to say that children should not be working in factories," Mr. Krugman said.

Not that most economists argue for sweatshops at home. The United States, they say, can afford to set much higher labor standards than poor countries—though Europe's are so high, some say, that high unemployment results.

Labor leaders and politicians who challenge sweatshops abroad say that they harm American workers as well, stealing jobs and lowering wages—a point that some economists dispute. "It is especially galling when American workers lose jobs to places where workers are really being exploited," said Mark Levinson, chief economist at the Union of Needletrades, Industrial and Textile Employees, who argues for trade sanctions to enforce global labor rules.

Yet when corporations voluntarily cut their ties to sweatshops, the victims can be the very same people sweatshop opponents say they want to help. In Honduras, where the legal working age is 14, girls toiled 75 hours a week for the 31-cent hourly minimum to make the Kathie Lee Gifford clothing line for Wal-Mart. When Wal-Mart canceled its contract, the girls lost their jobs and blamed Mrs. Gifford.

Mr. Krugman blames American self-righteousness, or guilt over Indonesian women and children sewing sneakers at 60 cents an hour. "A policy of good jobs in principle, but no jobs in practice, might assuage our consciences," he said, "but it is no favor to its alleged beneficiaries."

6

Child Labor Is Beneficial

Hannah Lapp

Hannah Lapp is a writer and farmer living in western New York.

Hard work benefits children because it enables them to experience joy through discovery and achievement. As with sports activities, hard work tests children's strength and endurance; it increases their sense of self-worth by allowing them to face difficult challenges and take responsibility for their actions. Children should be exposed to the character-building benefits of hard labor while they are young and receptive.

As a child growing up on a family-run dairy farm, I learned what the "hard" means in hard work before I turned 10. But my early experiences on the job also taught me the joy of achievement, and a rich array of lessons and skills that would prove invaluable to me in later life. That's why the term "child labor" doesn't automatically repulse me, except for the way modern usage has distorted it into a tool to deprive other youngsters of the treasures I myself found in hard work.

Work provides opportunity and discovery

Work was part of my life for as long as I can remember. Before school age, it was lighter tasks, such as helping with dishes so my older siblings could get to classes on time. At times I worked because Mom instructed me to do a particular job. More often, I followed my parents or older siblings around to help out with whatever they were doing, simply because it provided me with opportunity and discovery—two things children crave.

My parents expected us to pitch in with work not only because they considered it good for us, but because they needed us. They could not have provided for their 12 children on only our father's farm laborer income, and under no circumstances did they intend to accept government aid. Since the family's survival depended on our own efforts, we children grew up seeing ourselves as part of the big scheme of things.

My older brothers and sisters worked for many years in situations less ideal than the family farm setting I enjoyed in my childhood. Their long

Reprinted from Hannah Lapp, "A Defense of Child Labor," *The American Enterprise*, September/ October 1995, by permission of *The American Enterprise*, a Washington, D.C.–based magazine of politics, business, and culture.

days of hoeing or picking tomatoes under a blazing Arkansas sun during our family's migrant labor days were often difficult. So were the times when a parent or some of the children had to board away from home to follow a particular fruit-picking season.

I feel sorry for youngsters nowadays who are being told . . . that they're not supposed to do real work—the straining, grinding kind that tests your strength and helps pay the bills.

In 1967, one of those stormy years of scraping together toward a farm of our own, six of my older siblings managed a tomato harvest by themselves. Mom was tied down at home with the baby and Dad held a farm job, so my 15-year-old sister took charge of the young work force. For several weeks they boarded in a shanty on their employer's land, some 80 miles from home. Each one down to the youngest crew member, who was six, would toil from dawn to sunset in a back-breaking endeavor to fill as many baskets of tomatoes as he could.

Today my older siblings speak of those times with fondness rather than regret. It's partly because those very exertions were the ones that enabled us to reach the family dream of establishing our own farm. But it's more than that. It's because of the enormous sense of self-worth they discovered in meeting those challenges.

The lessons of labor

Perhaps people who can't comprehend the merits of hard work for children could begin to understand by correlating it to sports activities. Our society is quite accepting of the idea that youngsters should test their endurance, face rigorous competition, and even risk physical injury in the sports arena. No one thinks it odd that children should enjoy and benefit from these stressful activities.

Looking back, I can compare some of my youthful lust for work with other youngsters' enthusiasm for sports. The thrill of competing with peers and the glory of adult approval were big factors, just as they are in school ball games. But my own experiences have given me a bias in favor of work, where the glory is much less temporary.

The lessons work taught me came alive in my heart and hands, affecting my thought process like no amount of textbook study could. Be gentle with the heifer, or she'll be impossible to handle. Be responsible with that gate, or you'll be rudely awakened with cows out at night. Follow instructions and work hard when you're with the haying crew—otherwise you won't be included the next time. Get that row of cabbage weeded right, or you'll be doing it over again instead of having your break.

I feel sorry for youngsters nowadays who are being told by the adult world that they're not supposed to do real work—the straining, grinding kind that tests your strength and helps pay the bills. I'd like them to have a chance to discover the rewards of labor while they're young, adventuresome, and impressionable. My own workplace experience came early and was heavy, and I, for one, am grateful.

7

The United States Should Ban Imports of Products Made by Children

Tom Harkin

Tom Harkin, a Democratic senator from Iowa, is a member of the Committee on Labor and Human Resources and the Appropriations Committee. He has introduced a congressional bill, the Child Labor Deterrence Act, which would ban imports of goods produced by children.

The United States Congress should pass the proposed Child Labor Deterrence Act to help stop the exploitation of children by industrial and mining companies. This act would prohibit U.S. imports of goods produced by laborers under the age of fifteen; it would also urge world leaders to ensure an international trade ban on merchandise made by young children. Such legislation would help third world countries enforce laws against child labor; ultimately, it would protect the world's youngsters from the abusive and hazardous conditions often found in factories that rely on low-wage labor. As of November 1998, this legislation had not passed.

O ur laws prohibit the importation of ivory, endangered species such as the spotted turtle, and products made from prison labor. Yet, our laws fall silent when it comes to goods made through the exploitation of children. We look out for animals and prisoners, but fail to protect youngsters from exploitive and abusive labor.

This tragedy is of global proportions. The International Labor Organizations (ILO) reports that the number of children in abusive and oftentimes unsafe working conditions instead of school is increasing throughout the world. According to the ILO, those under the age of 15 constitute 11% of the workforce in some Asian countries and up to 26% in many Latin American nations. There are considerably more than 100,000,000 child laborers around the globe, many of whom work as bonded labor to repay debts owned by their parents. Some even are kidnapped or forced into labor.

Reprinted from Tom Harkin, "Put an End to the Exploitation of Child Labor," *USA Today* magazine, January 1996, by permission of the Society for the Advancement of Education, ©1996.

The scope of the problem

The problem of child labor was brought into greater focus during the recent Mexican Free Trade Agreement. In Mexico, 5-10,000,000 youngsters are employed illegally, often in hazardous jobs and making products for export to the U.S. Thirteen-year-old girls have been found working 48-hour weeks producing electric wiring strips for General Electric in Nogales and dashboard components for General Motors at its Delnosa plant.

In 1993, the U.S. Department of Labor investigated the use of exploitive and abusive child labor in goods imported to the U.S. The study, "By the Sweat and Toil of Children: The Use of Child Labor in American Imports," targeted 19 countries, where at least 46,000,000 youngsters work, many producing goods for the U.S. market. The report revealed a horrible picture of how children are contributing to their nation's export industry.

In Southeast Asia, where it is estimated that at least half of all child workers live, they toil 14-hour days in crowded factories and knot carpets for hours in dusty huts. American consumers buy more than 40% of India's carpet exports and account for over 50% of Bangladesh's earnings from garment exports.

Moreover, reports indicate that 10,000,000 of the 55,000,000 child workers in south Asia are bonded laborers. In Colombia, almost 800,000 children ages 12 through 17 are exposed to toxic substances as they process and harvest flowers for export.

Something needs to be done to discourage this practice. Children in developing countries, for the sake of their future and that of their economies, should be in schools and not in factories working long hours for little or no pay under hazardous conditions. That's why the Child Labor Deterrence Act was introduced in Congress, aimed at eliminating a major form of child abuse internationally. It attempts to curb poverty by getting these kids out of hazardous, abusive working conditions and into school where they may receive an education and contribute productively to their economy. It also seeks to raise the standard of living in the Third World and to assist those governments in enforcing their laws by not providing a market for goods made by children.

Banning imports of goods made by children

The Child Labor Deterrence Act would prohibit the importation of any product made in whole or in part by youngsters under 15 who are employed in industry or mining. The legislation is intended to strengthen existing U.S. trade legislation, as well as help Third World countries enforce their child labor laws. In fact, most nations where child labor is the biggest problem already have laws on the book against such exploitation, but they are not enforced.

In addition, the bill directs the U.S. Secretary of Labor to compile and maintain a list of foreign industries and their respective countries of origin that use child labor in the production of exports to the U.S. Once such a foreign industry has been identified, the Secretary of the Treasury is instructed to prohibit the entry of any of its goods. The entry ban would not apply if U.S. importers can certify that they took reasonable steps to ensure products were imported from identified industries not made by child labor. Reasonable steps include an exporter having entered into a contract with an independent nongovernmental organization (NGO) that is credible and capable of certifying that product is not made with child labor, affixing a licensed label certifying so, and requiring such proper certification and labeling by the importer in its purchase and supply order. In addition, Pres. Bill Clinton is being urged to seek an agreement with other governments to secure an international ban on trade in the goods made at the hands of kids.

This bill places no undue burden on U.S. importers. I do not believe that American consumers knowingly would buy products made with child labor, but, most often, they don't know. Moreover, no respectable importer, company, or department store willingly would promote the exploitation of children or have its image tainted by having word come out that goods sold are produced at the hands of child labor.

The [Child Labor Deterrence Act] is about protecting youngsters around the globe and their future from the physical and mental abuse that often accompany long hours of labor under hazardous circumstances.

Some would suggest that this legislation is unenforceable, that child labor is too hidden and difficult to locate, but this is not the case. Just as human rights organizations such as Amnesty International are able to document cases of human rights abuses and torture around the world, so can the identities of those industries and their host countries that are violating international labor standards by employing and exploiting children be identified. This legislation delineates the relative responsibilities of both importers and exporters with regard to the certification that a good not be a product of child labor. To a large extent, enforcement would be provided by the industry itself, as well as NGOs and other human rights, development, social, and religious organizations.

There are arguments from many groups claiming that youngsters would be worse off should this bill become a law. Some maintain that the legislation is merely punitive and will not address the underlying causes of child labor.

It is no secret that most children work because their families and their nations are poverty stricken. Nevertheless, while poverty may be the most significant cause of child labor, it is not the only one. For instance, many kids end up working because schools are unavailable, inadequate, or unaffordable. In many nations where child labor is prevalent, more money is spent and allocated for military expenditures than for education and health services. Human development and strong economies demand a healthy, productive, and well-educated populace.

Breaking the cycle of poverty

Employers prefer to employ children because they come cheap and are compliant. It's as simple as that. Child labor both causes and perpetuates poverty, as the worst instances of it are found where adult unemployment rates are high. The best way to break the cycle is by getting children out of factories and into schools, raising the standard of living in the Third World so nations can compete on the quality of goods and not on the misery or suffering of those who made them.

Another argument is that legislation which seeks to eliminate child labor imposes U.S. standards on the developing world. However, the proposed bill prevents certain manufacturers in developing countries that are exploiting children economically from imposing their standards on the U.S. and its consumers—not the other way around. Developing countries do not have to wait until poverty is eradicated before eliminating the exploitation of youngsters through child labor.

Some Asian nations—such as Sri Lanka, South Korea, and parts of India—successfully have concentrated on educating children, rather than putting them to work under abusive and exploitive circumstances. These countries have recognized that, in the long term, their economies will be competitive only with an educated, skilled, and healthy workforce.

Keep in mind the distinction between child work and exploitive child labor. The legislation does not bar children from selling newspapers, shining shoes, or working on the family farm, but, rather, prohibits work in the hazardous jobs of mining and industry under abusive and exploitive conditions.

This child labor legislation attempts to stop the economic exploitation of children and to get them out of the most dangerous jobs, such as industry and mining, by limiting the role of the U.S. in providing an open market for foreign goods made by underage kids. Other nations should do the same.

The bill is about protecting youngsters around the globe and their future from the physical and mental abuse that often accompany long hours of labor under hazardous circumstances. It is about protecting them from the immoral notion that a child of a particular social class is good only to toil and labor in factories and mines.

If the U.S. can protect animals and prisoners, the least it can do is to protect the world's children better.

Some organizations, corporations, and individuals have begun to take steps toward ameliorating this situation. The Child Labor Coalition, composed of more than 32 nongovernmental organizations, launched a U.S. consumer education campaign for the Rugmark—a label affixed to carpets from India, Pakistan, and Nepal, assuring customers that the product is not made with child labor. This helps to educate consumers and remind them that there are products made without child labor. Individuals have a choice and can make a difference.

The Swedish retailer Ikea decided not to carry carpets unless they can be certified as made without child labor. Companies such as Levi Strauss and Reebok have demanded that their overseas contractors only hire workers over the age of 14. The Bangladesh garment manufacturers and exporters association, along with UNICEF and the International Labor Organization (ILO), have agreed to place working children in an education program and implement an immediate ban on the further hiring of those under the age of 15.

Recently, I signed a letter with other members of Congress to the World Bank and International Monetary Fund addressing child labor concerns. We proposed that these institutions focus more on providing basic education, primary health, economic development, and labor protection for the poor. These international financial institutions should concentrate more on increasing access for poor people to productive resources that would allow them to end the cycle of poverty. Involving greater economic and social participation by those in poverty would spur economic growth and address the absolute poverty that is fueling political instability, environmental destruction, and soaring population.

I took my case to Geneva, Switzerland, in May, 1995, and met with top officials from the United Nations, General Agreement on Tariffs and Trade (GATT) talks, and the ILO to discuss child labor. Moreover, in April, 1995, my legislation and others similar to it gained the support of 112 Nobel Laureates when they established the Childright Worldwide organization, linking legislative and non-legislative initiatives to stop child exploitation.

It is time to consider trade issues with a moral, and not just monetary, dimension. The fight to end the worldwide exploitation of child labor will continue. Americans one day should be able to enjoy fully the goods they purchase, knowing that they were not made at the expense of youngsters who worked in abusive and exploitive conditions. If the U.S. can protect animals and prisoners, the least it can do is to protect the world's children better.

Efforts to Ban Goods Made by Children Are Counterproductive

Shahidul Alam

Shahidul Alam is a photographer, writer, and activist who runs the Drik Picture Library in Dhaka, Bangladesh.

Efforts to discourage the use of child labor include a congressional bill, first introduced in 1992 by Democratic Senator Tom Harkin, which would ban the importation of products made by children. Such legislation is counterproductive. Children factory workers in third world countries contribute needed income to their households, and these children face increased poverty or more exploitative work conditions if new regulations force them to leave their factory jobs. Such was the case in Bangladesh in 1994, when thousands of children lost their factory jobs after news of the Harkin bill aired. Activists who truly want to improve the lives of working children must carefully analyze the complex social realities surrounding the issue of child labor.

Editor's Note: The children's names in this viewpoint have been changed to protect them.

No. No photographs. Saleha is scared. Many a time she has hidden under tables, been locked up in the toilet, or been sent to the roof in the scorching sun for two or three hours. It happens whenever foreign buyers enter the factory. She knows she is under-age, and doesn't want photographers messing things up—she needs the job. The whole industry has suddenly become sensitive. Owners want their factories open. The workers want their jobs. The special schools for former child labourers want aid money. No photographs.

Neither Saleha nor any of the other child workers I have interviewed have ever heard of Senator Tom Harkin. All they know is that pressure

Reprinted from Shahidul Alam, "Thank You, Mr. Harkin, Sir!" *The New Internationalist*, July 1997, by permission of the Guardian News Service, London.

from the U.S. which buys most of Bangladesh's garments, has resulted in thousands of them losing their jobs at a stroke.

According to a press release by the garment employers in October 1994: '50,000 children lost their jobs because of the Harkin Bill.' A UNICEF worker confirms 'the jobs went overnight'.

The controversial bill, the 'Child Labor Deterrence Act', had first been introduced in 1992. A senior International Labour Organization (ILO) official has no doubt that the original bill was put forward 'primarily to protect US trade interests'—Tom Harkin is sponsored by a key US trade union, and cheap imports from the Third World were seen as undercutting American workers' jobs. 'When we all objected to this aspect of the Bill,' says the ILO official, 'which included a lot of resistance in the US, the Bill was amended, the trading aspect was toned down, and it was given a humanitarian look.' It was when it was reintroduced after these amendments in 1993 that the Bill had its devastating impact in Bangladesh.

Humanitarian concern?

The child workers themselves find it particularly hard to interpret the US approach as one of 'humanitarian concern'. When asked why the buyers have been exerting such pressure against child labour, Moyna, a ten-year-old orphan who has just lost her job, comments: They loathe us, don't they? We are poor and not well educated, so they simply despise us. That is why they shut the factories down.' Moyna's job had supported her and her grandmother but now they must both depend on relatives.

Other children have had no alternative but to seek new kinds of work. When UNICEF and the ILO made a series of follow-up visits they found that the children displaced from the garment factories were working at stone-crushing and street hustling—more hazardous and exploitative activities than their factory jobs.

'It is easier for the boys to get jobs again,' Moyna complains, pointing to ex-garment boys who have jobs in welding and bicycle factories. Girls usually stay at home, doing household work and looking after smaller children; many end up getting married simply to ease money problems.

> *The child workers themselves find it particularly hard to interpret the US approach as one of "humanitarian concern."*

In the wake of the mass expulsion of child garment workers it was plain that something had gone very wrong. UNICEF and the ILO tried to pick up the pieces. After two years of hard talking with the garment employers they came up with a Memorandum of Understanding. This guaranteed that no more children under 14 would be hired, that existing child workers would be received into special schools set up by local voluntary organizations and would receive a monthly stipend to compensate them for the loss of their wages.

Some garment owners feel that, instead of doing a deal, they should have called the US bluff and continued employing young children. 'We export 150 million shirts a year to the US,' says one. 'The K-mart $12 shirt would have cost $24. Bill Clinton would have lost his job.'

As of 1997 10,547 of the estimated 50,000 children have been registered, and of these 8,067 have enlisted in school. Most weren't registered initially, as few garment owners admitted having children working in their factories. Many lost their jobs before the registration process began. Unregistered children, regardless of their age or their schooling, are not admitted into the scheme.

Saleha is tall for her age. Though in her factory there are quite a few under-age children, in most factories children that look small are no longer taken. This is what Moyna and Ekram and the other children repeatedly say: 'We didn't make the size.' In a country where births are not registered there is no way of accurately determining a person's age. Children with good growth keep their jobs. Children who look smaller, perhaps because they are malnourished, do not.

Sabeena's story

The reliance on size rather than age means that many children are still at work in the factories—and many have no inclination to take up a place in one of the special schools. Take Sabeena. Her factory is colourful with tinsel when I visit and many of the girls have glitter on their faces. It is the Bangla New Year and Eid all in one and they are celebrating. Sabeena proudly shows me the machine she works on. She is almost 14 and, like Saleha, big for her age. She has been working at a garment factory ever since she finished Grade Five, about 18 months prior to my factory visit. Until then, schooling was free. There was no way her parents could pay for her to go to school and, with her father being poorly, Sabeena needed to work to keep the family going.

Taking home 2,200 take ($52) a month (with overtime) Sabeena, at 13, is now the main breadwinner in the family. She is lucky to have work, though she would rather study. She laughs when I talk of her going to school. She has mouths to feed, and to give up her job for a 300-taka-per-month stipend for going to school simply wouldn't make sense. Besides, the special schools only teach up to Grade Five. The better students, who have studied that far, find they have neither jobs nor seats in the school. So Sabeena's studies begin at around eleven at night, with a paid private tutor, usually by candlelight. At seven in the morning she has to leave for work. Seven days a week.

Money is a key concern even for those children who have been received into the special schools. At the school run by the Bangladesh Rural Advancement Committee (BRAC) in Mirpur, the children gather round a worker doing the rounds. 'When do we get paid, sir?' they keep asking.

Despite the promises, not a single child that I have interviewed has received the full pay they are owed. In some cases field workers, eager to improve their admission rates, have promised considerably more than the stipulated 300 take ($7) per month. In others, unfounded rumours have created expectations that the schools cannot meet.

Shahjahan was one of the lucky ones admitted to a BRAC school. The

300 take per month is a small sum for him too, but he works in a tailoring shop from nine till eleven in the morning, and again from two-thirty in the afternoon till ten at night. He doesn't complain. Though the scheme does not encourage it, he feels he is getting the best of both worlds: free schooling, including a stipend, as well as paid work and a potential career.

Did they like working in garment factories? The children find this a strange question. They earned money because of it, and it gave them a certain status that non-working children did not have. They put up with the long hours. The exceptions remind me that it is children we are talking about. 'I cried when they forced me to do overtime on Thursday nights,' says Moyna. 'That was when they showed *Alif Laila* (Arabian Nights) on TV.'

Child workers are popular with factory owners. 'Ten-to-twelve-year-olds are the best,' says Farooq, the manager of Sabeena's factory. 'They are easier to control, not interested in men, or movies, and obedient.' He forgets to mention that they are not unionized and that they agree to work for 500 take ($12) per month when the minimum legal wage for a helper is 930 take.

The realities of garment workers' lives

Owners see Tom Harkin as a well-meaning soul with little clue about the realities of garment workers' lives. 'As a student, I too hailed the Bill,' says Sohel, the production manager at Captex Garments. I was happy that someone was fighting for children's rights. But now that I work in a factory and have to turn away these children who need jobs. I see things differently. Sometimes I take risks and, if a child is really in a bad way, I let them work, but it is dangerous.'

The notion that a garment employer might be helping children by allowing them to work may seem very strange to people in the West. But in a country where the majority of people live in villages where children work in the home and the fields as part of growing up, there are no romantic notions of childhood as an age of innocence. Though children are cared for, childhood is seen as a period for learning employable skills. Children have always helped out with family duties. When this evolves into a paid job in the city neither children nor their families see it as anything unusual. In poor families it is simply understood that everyone has to work.

In poor families it is simply understood that everyone has to work.

The money that children earn is generally handed over to parents, who run the household as best as they can. Most parents want their children to go to school. But they also feel that schooling is a luxury they cannot afford. The garment industry has increased the income of working-class families in recent years and this has also led to a change in attitudes. Many middle-class homes now complain that it is difficult to get domestic 'help' as working-class women and children choose to work in garment factories rather than as servants. This choice—made on the grounds not just of better economics, but of greater self-respect—is one many children have lost because of the Harkin Bill.

To address child labour without addressing exploitation is to treat the symptom, not the disease.

The US is wielding power without responsibility. A nation with a history of genocide and slavery, and a reputation for being a bully in international politics, suddenly proclaims itself a champion of people's rights, but refuses to make concessions over the rates it will pay. The dollar price-tags on the garments produced in some factories suggest a vast profit being made at the US end. The buyers claim that what they pay for the garments is determined by 'market forces'. The garment owners make the same claim with regard to the conditions of employment for their workers. Both are simply justifying their own version of exploitation—and to address child labour without addressing exploitation is to treat the symptom, not the disease.

The garment-industry experience has led to an active debate amongst development workers and child-rights activists. 'What we have done here in Bangladesh is described as fantastic,' says a senior ILO worker. 'I wonder how fantastic it really is. How much difference will these two or three years in school make to these children? In three years, the helper could have been an operator, with better pay and more savings. Even if the manufacturers keep their word and give them back their jobs at the end of their schooling, the Memorandum children will hardly be better off, while their peers will have gotten on with their careers. We have spent millions of dollars on 8,000 children. The money itself could have transformed their lives. This is an experiment by the donors, and the Bangladeshi children have to pay.'

Consumer Pressure Can Reduce the Use of Sweatshops

Linda F. Golodner

Linda F. Golodner is president of the National Consumers League, an organization that works to bring consumer power to bear on market and labor issues.

Consumer pressure can effectively reduce the use of sweatshop labor and child labor. Early in the twentieth century, consumer groups helped to bring about the implementation of labor standards in the United States that abolished child labor, required a minimum wage, and protected the right to collective bargaining. In the 1990s, several companies responded to consumer outrage against sweatshops by establishing corporate codes of conduct—rules that ban the abusive treatment of workers in manufacturing plants. Although these codes have been inconsistently enforced, they set the groundwork for the Apparel Industry Partnership, a coalition of concerned garment companies, unions, and human rights organizations. This coalition is developing an industry-wide standard of conduct that prohibits exploitative work conditions. Furthermore, persistent consumer activism has led several cities to adopt resolutions banning the sale of sweatshop-made goods.

L ong before consumers united for product, food, and drug safety and myriad other issues with direct consumer impact, they cast their influence unselfishly to improve conditions for the workers who produced the nation's goods.

The 1890s was a time when industrialization in the United States burgeoned, where workers eked out an existence on starvation wages. Corporations—replacing family firms, partnerships, and proprietorships—showed little interest in those they employed. Cheap labor made higher profits, and profit was the name of the game.

The consumers movement was founded on the belief that the cus-

Reprinted from Linda F. Golodner, "Apparel Industry Code of Conduct: A Consumer Perspective on Responsibility," a paper presented at the Notre Dame Center for Ethics and Religious Values in Business, October 6, 1997, by permission of the author.

tomer who bought sweatshop goods was as much the employer of sweated labor as the boss of the shop. Consumers leagues became the central force in the social justice movement.

"It is the duty of consumers to find out under what conditions the articles they purchase are produced and distributed and to insist that these conditions shall be wholesome and consistent with a respectable existence·on the part of the workers." Josephine Shaw Lowell, founder New York City Consumers League, 1891.

For over ninety years, the National Consumers League (NCL) has represented consumers who are concerned about the conditions under which products are manufactured. To illustrate the philosophy, an early League motto was the following: *To live means to buy, to buy means to have power, to have power means to have duties.*

The consumers movement was founded on the belief that the customer who bought sweatshop goods was as much the employer of sweated labor as the boss of the shop.

In July 1940, Mary Dublin described the League's work as "an expression of the conviction that consumers have a far-reaching responsibility to use their buying power and their power as citizens to advance the general welfare of the community. Substandard wages and depressed industrial conditions impose a burden not on labor alone but on consumers as well. What is not paid in wages, the community is called upon to pay in relief; in wage subsidies; in contributions to meet the cost of illness, dependency, delinquency, and numerous other social ills which these conditions produce."

Since those early years, the consumers movement has blossomed into many areas of interest—from food/product standards and quality to consumer rights to consumer protection and more. New consumer organizations have expanded the scope and definition of consumer. But the consumer movement's history and mission (for some like the National Consumers League) reflect the continuing commitment and sense of responsibility for the conditions under which products are produced and for the decisions consumers make in the marketplace.

> Fifty years ago today a brilliant, though basically simple, idea was born. This was that the people who buy goods in stores could have a say as to the conditions under which those goods were produced. By their economic and political pressure they could fight child labor, they could protect women against exploitation, they could make the ideal of the minimum wage a living fact. (editorial excerpt on the NCL from the *New York Times,* December 9, 1949).

Consumer pressure significantly influenced the U.S. passage of child labor laws, minimum wage, and overtime compensation, as well as shorter work days and work weeks. Such efforts culminated in 1938's Fair Labor Standards Act. The League's nearly one hundred years of experience in fighting sweatshops and child labor underscores some basic truths which are applicable today:

1. Consumers should not expect a problem to be solved just because a law has been passed. When various industries, responding to the National Industrial Recovery Act of 1933, established codes prescribing maximum hours, minimum wages, collective bargaining, and abolition of child labor, the National Consumers League hoped its major work was accomplished. When the codes went into effect, the League kept in close touch with workers to find out how they were affected. It was soon apparent that in industries where unions were strong, workers benefitted through higher wages and shorter hours. But in unorganized industries, while there was improvement in hours and wages, unscrupulous employers used every possible device to rob workers of what was due them legally. (On May 27, 1935, the U.S. Supreme Court declared the Act unconstitutional.)

2. Consumers want an uncomplicated, easy means to identify products made under decent conditions. As consumer demand increased for such products during the early 1900s, the League developed and oversaw the use of the White Label. The label was attached to women's and children's stitched cotton underwear if the factory guaranteed that it obeyed all factory laws, made all goods on the premises, required no overtime work, and employed no children under age 16. Representatives of the League inspected factories to assure compliance. Originating in New York City, use of the label spread to 13 states. In 1918, the League discontinued the label as union leaders began developing labels that guaranteed labor standards enforcement. Consumers see labels as an easy point-of-purchase tool to use in the marketplace.

The concluding years of the 20th century have witnessed the expansion of the global marketplace and the propelling of companies to a transnational playing field. The consumers movement has responded with increased action and awareness outside of its own national borders to consider social responsibility on a global level.

Media and consumer outrage over child labor and sweatshops spurred many companies to initial action within the last decade.

Consumers who are educated about exploitative working conditions and feel a sense of responsibility to act upon this knowledge find frustration in the marketplace. As a reaction to a lack of information and labels to help the conscientious consumer identify products made under decent conditions, many consumers are taking personal action—to include even personal boycotts of certain products, companies, and countries.

Some detractors claim that personal boycotts are doomed to failure through lack of massive consumer participation. The facts, however, suggest that consumers choose a personal boycott as a means of expression because they find a company's, industry's or nation's policies or behavior morally objectionable. In other words, their personal action is based on their commitment to not be an accomplice, even with a few dollars, in support of offensive policies. Thus it is not the consumer's worry whether their action will similarly motivate other consumers, but it justly can be the worry of the offending company, industry, or country.

According to the 1997 Human Rights Watch survey, "Because the goods purchased in one country may be produced by victims of repression in another, the very act of consumption can be seen as complicity in that repression." The expansion of the global economy is creating "new and immediate connections among distant people," and is thereby spawning "a surprising new source of support for the human-rights cause." To avoid personal complicity, many consumers "are insisting on guarantees that they are not buying the products of abusive labor conditions."

Over the years, consumer activism has influenced many industries. The results have been new product offerings, new labels, and new packaging. For example, the automobile industry was disinterested, often hostile, to providing airbags, anti-lock brakes, and other safety features until consumer demand necessitated their change of heart.

An informed, empowered, and energized consumer movement is responsible for much of the progress against sweatshops and child labor abuses.

Consumer pressure for more healthy alternatives in fast food restaurants has culminated in consumers being able to go into any McDonald's today and get a salad. Consumers wanted more nutrition information on packaged foods—especially detailed fat and saturated fat information—and they got it.

These examples reinforce the tremendous power that consumers have over industry. The same influence has been and can continue to provide improvements in social issues such as child labor and sweatshop exploitation.

Karl E. Meyer raised an interesting analogy to today's consumer efforts at social responsibility (Editorial Notebook, the *New York Times,* June 28, 1997).

> As Hong Kong reverted to China on July 1, 1997, we were reminded of a bit of history known as the Opium War between Britain and China from 1839 to 1842. Western protests against the war mark it as the beginning of a concern with international human rights. Along with the slave trade, the traffic in opium was the dirty underside of an evolving global trading economy.
>
> In America as in Europe, pretty much everything was deemed fair in the pursuit of profits. In 1839, the Emperor of China responded to the epidemic addiction to opium in his country by naming an Imperial Commissioner to end the trade, which in a large part was conducted by American companies, which brought opium from India to China through Turkey. Outrage was expressed by British and

American press and the pulpit, forcing the businesses to pull
out of the opium trade.

We no longer believe that anything goes in the global marketplace, regardless of social consequences. It is precisely
this conviction that underlies efforts to attach human rights
conditions to trading relations—to temper the amorality of
the market.

The shortcomings of industry codes of conduct

Media and consumer outrage over child labor and sweatshops spurred
many companies to initial action within the last decade. In the early
1990s, industry leaders who developed corporate codes of conduct (primarily targeting their overseas contractors) were Levi Strauss, Reebok, and
Liz Claiborne. Other companies followed, each emphasizing its own list
of abusive practices that it would not tolerate.

On several levels, the company codes of conduct proved problematic.
They fell short of their intentions, and thus lost their credibility among
consumers.

Variation between company codes and standards bred confusion: Using
child labor as an example as it is one of the issues most commonly addressed in codes of conduct, compare these differing definitions and per-
ceptions of child labor:

- Levi Strauss says child labor is not acceptable and defines a "child"
  as a person under the age of 14 or who is under the compulsory
  schooling age.
- Wal-Mart will not accept the use of child labor in the manufacture
  of goods which it sells. Suppliers/subcontractors must not recruit
  persons under the age of 15 or below the compulsory schooling
  age. If national legislation includes higher criteria, these must be
  applied.
- JC Penney will not allow the importation into the U.S. of merchandise manufactured by illegal child labor.
- The Gap states that no person under the age of 14 may be allowed
  to work in a factory that produces Gap Inc. goods and that vendors
  must comply with local child labor laws.
- The FIFA (soccer ball governing body) code refers to child labor in
  the terms of International Labor Organization (ILO) Convention
  138 (i.e., children under 15 years of age, as well as provisions for
  younger children in certain countries).

In word only, not in deed: Despite the introduction of codes of conduct,
company implementation for the most part has been ill-conceived and ill-
executed. Media reports, worker complaints, and persistent consumer
concerns have underscored the ineffectiveness of the company monitored
codes of conduct. It has become evident that words on paper and even the
best intentioned internal monitoring is unreliable and inadequate.

Lack of transparency: Absent assurances from independent monitors
and publicly available reports, consumers have little assurance that company codes of conduct are being meaningfully implemented and overseen.

Child labor exploitation is a global issue—with problems evident in over two-thirds of all nations. According to a 1997 report by the International Labor Organization, more than 250 million children between the ages of five and fourteen are forced to work in 100 countries, most performing dangerous tasks. Ninety-five percent of all child workers live in developing countries. In some regions, as many as 25 percent of children between the ages of 10 and 14 are estimated to be working. The Department of State's 1991 and 1992 Human Rights Reports and a 1992 ILO report attest to the growing numbers of children in servitude and their worsening conditions of work.

The problem is growing along with the expansion of the global marketplace. Child labor is cheap labor. Children are targeted for non-skilled, labor intensive work. Docile and easily controlled, employers have no fear of children demanding rights or organizing. Child employment instead of adult employment creates a climate where many children support their unemployed or underemployed parents and the entire family and their future families remain in poverty, ignorance, and exploitation.

Child labor flourishes under many conditions—cultural traditions; prejudice and discrimination based on gender, ethnic, religious or racial issues; unavailability of educational and other alternatives for working children; and no or weak enforcement of compulsory education and child labor laws. Globalization is strengthening child labor through providing ready access to areas of cheap labor that are rife with the above described conditions. Child labor increasingly offers an attractive incentive to keep labor costs down in a highly competitive global market.

Many U.S. companies have included child labor in their codes of conduct, due to persistent evidence of child exploitation in the industry. Although no definitive figures are available on the number of children working in the garment industry, the U.S. Department of Labor's Child Labor Study (1994) identified children working in the garment industry in most of the countries they reviewed. A direct connection was evident between these countries' exports and the United States, the world's largest importer of garments from 168 countries. "Child labor" does not refer to children working on the family farm or in the family business. It refers to employment that prevents school attendance, and which is often performed under conditions which are hazardous or harmful to children.

The apparel industry code of conduct

In 1996, President Bill Clinton convened a meeting at the White House, inviting apparel industry leaders, unions, and non-governmental organizations to form a task force on sweatshops. The President charged the group to determine appropriate steps for the industry to take "to ensure that the products they make and sell are manufactured under decent and humane working conditions." He also charged the group to "develop options to inform consumers that the products they buy are not produced under those exploitative conditions."

The Apparel Industry Partnership's negotiations and first report revolved around the development of an industry standard code of conduct. The code blends elements of existing corporate codes into a set of standards which may be adopted by the apparel industry as a whole. Definitions of each prohibition related to child labor, maximum work weeks, harassment and abuse, forced labor, and other issues, were hammered out. Integral to the code is definitive monitoring, including both internal and external (i.e., independent) evaluations of compliance.

The Partnership is working to establish a permanent association that will provide participation by companies that adopt the code of conduct, as well as setting the parameters of monitoring. It will also standardize and control the use of any symbol, label or other mechanism employed to provide information to the consumer about decent working conditions.

To ensure consumer confidence and the integrity of the governing association, several elements must be maintained in this initiative:

- Consumers want a "sweatshop free," "good labor practices," or "member of" claim that applies to both domestic and international production. Consumers are not going to react favorably to a company which is applauded for a sweatshop-free stand in the U.S. while doing business overseas with sweatshops.
- Consumers want a claim that is credible. Legitimate external, independent monitoring is essential for consumers to have confidence in any company claim.
- Consumers want the industry to work with their subcontractors who are found to be out of compliance with the code of conduct to assure that the problems are solved and restitution to the workers is made. Canceling contracts does not help workers.
- Consumers want easy access to information to enable ethical decision making, preferably at point of purchase.
- Consumers want full disclosure of manufacturers' performance in relation to the code of conduct.

Labels: easy access to information for consumers

Consumers have expanding choices in the global marketplace. Savvy shoppers ask questions and the answers often are the foundation for their purchasing decisions. Many consumers want to know what they are getting—and what they are supporting—when they buy.

The most obvious response of the savvy shopper is their burgeoning demand for labels. Consumers wanted more nutrition labeling on food and got it. The ever evident recycling symbol was a response to consumer concerns about environmental issues. Some consumers wanted dolphin safe tuna or products not tested on animals and the affected industries scrambled to provide assurances to consumers.

In the last few years, there has been a resurgence in interest for a label that identifies decent labor conditions. Country of origin and Made in USA labeling is an important beginning point. But, such labels do not provide the complete story behind the labor. Consumers want information, guarantees, and a choice in products made under decent conditions.

Whether to educate consumers about nutrition, environmental impact, product testing, or labor conditions, consumers expect labels to be meaningful and honest. A meaningful label for products made under decent labor conditions must delineate precisely what is meant and met by the use of the label. Consumers expect an honest label, where the veracity of the claim is assured through independent evaluation and oversight of the company or industry using the label.

One of the most credible labeling programs is RUGMARK. This trailblazing initiative certifies carpet manufacturers who meet stringent requirements to assure that no child labor is used in handmade carpets from India and Nepal. Consumer confidence in the label is gained through systematic independent monitoring and unannounced inspections of manufacturers by non-industry RUGMARK representatives. There are more than 1,000 children in RUGMARK-supported schools in India and Nepal. RUGMARK carpets represent nearly 15 percent of all Indian production and nearly 70 percent of Nepalese production. Pakistan is expected to form a RUGMARK program in 1998.

Other consumer efforts

An informed, empowered, and energized consumer movement is responsible for much of the progress against sweatshops and child labor abuses. In January 1996, the National Consumers League and the Union of Needletrades, Industrial and Textile Employees (UNITE) launched a Stop Sweatshop campaign, targeting both domestic and international sweatshops. The campaign's combined outreach represents over 50 million consumers. One goal of the Stop Sweatshops campaign is to equip consumers with the tools they need to send a "No Sweatshop" message to retailers and manufacturers.

"No Sweatshops" has gained new energy as public officials, city councils, and united consumers force the issue into the limelight in their hometown. Recognizing the advantages of citizen action and the greater responsiveness of local government, a new pressure point has been added to end sweatshop abuses. "If we can envision ourselves as a community of consumers rather than autonomous shoppers," says the Clean Clothes Campaign, "some remarkable things can happen."

Bangor's Clean Clothes Campaign: A city of nearly 31,000 residents, Bangor, Maine is working toward "sweatshop free" clothing within its city limits. Led by Peace through Interamerican Community Action, the Clean Clothes Campaign wants the city of Bangor to support a simple principle: Clothes sold in our community should not be supplied by manufacturers who violate established international standards regarding forced labor, child labor, poverty wages, and decent working conditions. They accomplished this in 1997 by banning the sale in Bangor of any item of clothing produced in violation of these most basic standards of ethical practice.

The campaign will next build upon the community consensus against sweatshops with a retailer campaign. Retailers will be pressed to take a pledge of corporate and social accountability to the Bangor community. The Clean Clothes Campaign insists that "ordinary people should have something to say about the behavior of businesses, large or small, that operate in our community. We would never permit local vendors to sell us rotten meat, or stolen property, or illicit drugs because such behavior offends our community values. Likewise, we do not condone international corporations supplying our retailers with items made under conditions that equally offend our sense of decency."

"FoulBall" spurs Los Angeles: The City Council of Los Angeles, California approved a resolution in December 1996, requiring the city to only

purchase sporting goods that have been certified by a reputable independent organization as having been manufactured without the illegal use of child labor. The resolution has received tremendous support from youth soccer leagues, parents, and schools.

The effort was a response to the FoulBall Campaign to end the exploitation of children in the manufacture of sports equipment. It has become a model resolution for other cities.

The heart and soul of the consumers movement is social responsibility.

Innovative Law in North Olmsted, Ohio: In February 1996, the North Olmsted City Council approved an ordinance forbidding the purchase, rent, or lease of goods which have been manufactured under sweatshop conditions. The law refers to the following when determining sweatshop conditions: child labor, forced labor, wages and benefits, hours of work, worker rights, and health and safety. A Cleveland suburb with a population of 35,000, North Olmsted's purchasing amounts to approximately $150,000 per year on items commonly produced in sweatshops.

Suppliers must sign a new clause on all contracts and purchase requisitions stating that their products are not made in sweatshops. If the city discovers a supplier does sell sweatshop products, the contract will be canceled or other appropriate action taken.

Twelve other cities in Ohio, including Cleveland and Dayton, have passed the same resolution. In Pennsylvania, Allentown has passed a law and Pittsburgh and Philadelphia are pending. Cities elsewhere who have the same law are San Francisco and Lansing. The North Olmsted model will be presented as a resolution urging all cities to adopt this policy at the annual U.S. Conference of Mayors meeting in January, 1998.

A look ahead

The Fiscal Year 1998 Treasury-Postal Appropriations, recently passed in Congress, contains a clarification of the Tariff Act of 1930. The law bans the import of items manufactured by "prison," "forced," or "indentured" labor. Congress has clarified in the Appropriations legislation that this prohibition includes forced and indentured child labor, as well as bonded child labor.

The clarifying language and subsequent enforcement by U.S. Customs is expected to impact nearly $100 million of imports. The effect it will have on the garment industry—and other industries—remains to be seen. There is no doubt, however, that this clarification poses a significant first step in closing down the U.S. market to products made through child labor exploitation.

Meanwhile, two other bills have been introduced in this Congress related to imports of products made by children. The Child Labor Free Consumer Information Act of 1997 (H.R. 1301 and S. 554) establishes a *voluntary* labeling system for wearing apparel and sporting goods made without child labor. The Child Labor Deterrence Act (H.R. 1328 and S. 332) would prohibit the importation of manufactured and mined goods into the United States which are produced by children under the age of 15.

The heart and soul of the consumers movement is social responsibility. Sweatshops and child labor are not new concerns nor a new battle for consumers. Our expectations in company conduct are reasonable and attainable, despite the complexities of global sourcing. And, like our predecessors, we will not give up the fight until consumers—at a minimum—are given a clear and credible choice in the marketplace for products made under decent conditions. No excuses accepted.

10

Efforts to Reduce the Use of Sweatshops Are Misguided

Irwin M. Stelzer

Irwin M. Stelzer is the director of regulatory policy studies at the American Enterprise Institute, a conservative think tank.

Attempts to reduce the use of overseas sweatshops are misguided. The effort on the part of trade unions and government officials to raise wages and to have goods manufactured under humane conditions would greatly increase production costs, driving many overseas plants out of business. This, in turn, would hurt the economies of developing nations and irrevocably damage international trade. Moreover, laborers in foreign factories are grateful for their jobs and generally are willing to work for wages that seem low by American standards. These wages are often higher than what overseas workers could earn in non-factory jobs. Consumers must recognize that the economic development of poor nations takes time and cannot be induced by banning the use of sweatshop labor.

First stop, San Francisco. All is changed. Where one of my favorite cigar stores once stood, a construction crew is at work on a new NikeTown. Then to Los Angeles, and a stroll down Beverly Hills's posh Wilshire Boulevard. A mob scene, with four policemen organizing the eager customers into lines that stretch around the block. The occasion: the grand opening of yet another NikeTown. And the beat goes on: A $100 million NikeTown is scheduled to open on Manhattan's East 57th Street within the next few months.

In a studio ten blocks uptown, Kathie Lee Gifford holds forth on live television every morning. Remember her embarrassment at discovering that a line of clothing bearing her name was being sewn by underpaid workers here and in Honduras? And her subsequent, tearfully contrite appearance before a congressional committee while husband Frank Gifford distributed cash to the exploited workers in New York City?

Let's move from Kathie Lee Gifford to Michael Jordan. In 1996, Jor-

Reprinted from Irwin M. Stelzer, "Niketown Shantytowns?" *The Weekly Standard*, September 16, 1996, by permission of the *Weekly Standard*.

dan signed a one-year contract for $25 million, a sum likely to be doubled by the fees he will receive for endorsing Nike sneakers and other products. Meanwhile, the workers who make the sneakers that bear his imprimatur earn only a few dollars a day. Jordan's critics like to point out that the Chicago Bulls' star earns more per minute of play than a Nike worker earns in a decade.

The overseas labor market

The triumph of the NikeTown stores, the discomfort of Kathie Lee Gifford, and the $12,500 a minute Michael Jordan earns are directly related. They involve the manufacture of goods for sale to American consumers by overseas workers who are paid far less than their American counterparts. These overseas workers are employed by contractors and subcontractors in Indonesia and elsewhere. The contractors are paid by American companies to manufacture everything from T-shirts for The Gap to sneakers for Nike.

The overseas manufacturers are tapping into a labor market in which a surplus of workers gives them superior bargaining power. They are dealing with a work force eager for jobs and capable of living on wages far lower than those paid to American workers. Not only is the pay low by the standards of the industrialized world, but the working conditions are, to American eyes, appalling. Air conditioning and other amenities taken for granted here are nonexistent; overtime work is mandatory, and holidays are few. By transferring work to parts of the world where production costs are a fraction of those at home, America's corporate chieftains can lay off expensive American workers and reward themselves with large bonuses as their companies profit.

So says a new coalition that wants to force American firms to change the way they do business overseas. First, of course, we have the trade unions, understandably eager to reduce the competition their members face from their counterparts in developing countries. Just as union organizers of old found that they had to follow the textile industry when it began its move from highly unionized and high-cost New England to the South if they were to protect their hard-won gains in the North, so today's union leaders would like to follow American manufacturers to Indonesia, Central America, and other places in which goods are being turned out for the American market. But they can't.

For one thing, those countries do not exactly roll out the welcome mat for union organizers, both because their regimes are hostile to the development of non-governmental power centers and because they recognize that the road to economic development is paved with foreign investment. For another, workers in those countries are not eager to antagonize employers who generally pay them far more than they can earn elsewhere, twice the minimum wage in Nike's case.

Attempts to rally consumers

Unable to organize the overseas work force they think has kept real wages in the U.S. apparel industry at sweatshop levels, trade-union leaders now want to persuade American consumers not to buy products made under supposedly substandard conditions. Just as Cesar Chavez once enlisted consumers in a boycott of grapes on behalf of farm workers, so today's unions are trying to enlist consumers in their battle to stem the tide of foreign-made goods. So far, they have found two allies.

The first is a diverse and as yet ineffective group of consumers that feels it is immoral for rich American companies to employ foreign workers, more often than not young women, at low pay for long hours in hot factories. One such protester ruefully describes his effort to stem the tide of customers waiting impatiently to flood a Nike store about to open in Seattle. Despite his highly informative sign, none of those lined up to charge the counters at the opening bell decided that solidarity with overseas workers was more important than a new pair of Air Jordans.

Their second ally has more clout. Led by labor secretary Robert Reich, the American government is putting pressure on the World Trade Organization (WTO) to "harmonize" global labor standards. The idea is simple: Require goods being sold on world markets to be manufactured under comparable conditions. The protectionist nature of this gambit is shown by the nature of its primary supporter, France, whose high-cost welfare state is threatened by competition from the developing countries. (France, by the way, fought every liberalizing feature of the last General Agreement on Tariffs and Trade agreement, places quotas on the importation of American films and music, and has managed its own economy into a 12.5 percent unemployment rate—and rising.)

[Overseas manufacturers] are dealing with a work force eager for jobs and capable of living on wages far lower than those paid to American workers.

But if wages and working conditions in every country were the same, if environmental regulations were identical, and if tax rates around the world were "harmonized," there would be very little international trade. For, as the Clinton administration well knows, international trade is basically a process by which countries with a comparative advantage in some aspect of the production process sell things to countries with an advantage in some other aspect.

So far, the administration has pressed its case at the WTO with little fanfare. But if Bill Clinton wins a second term, he will have good reason to pursue this subtly protectionist line with renewed vigor. For, beholden to the unions for the tens of millions of dollars they will have poured into his campaign coffers, the president will have to deliver training programs, time off to cope with family problems, time off in lieu of overtime, and other items on labor's wish list. But he will have little or no money to spend, and so he will have to impose the costs of these programs on businesses. [Clinton won a second term and supported anti-sweatshop policies.]

But that will make it even more difficult for domestic manufacturers to compete with overseas producers—unless those producers, too, are required to bear the costs of similar benefits. Enter the World Trade Organization and the administration's plea for "harmonization." This neat bit of policy wonkery doesn't sound protectionist—nothing as crude as tariff walls or import quotas. And it transfers income from consumers, who are too many to notice and too unorganized to complain, to a few union workers by imposing higher prices on the former to support higher wages for the latter.

Policy changes could harm overseas workers

American consumers will not be the only ones to suffer. Overseas workers struggling to emerge from poverty will also pay a steep price. One campaigner-against-exploitation boasted to me of having forced a retail chain to stop using "young teenage girls" to manufacture clothing for distribution in its U.S. stores. When asked what she thought those now-unemployed Salvadoran youngsters were doing, she responded that she assumed they were back in school! More likely, they are working at still lower wages, under still worse conditions, perhaps in occupations with more damaging long-run consequences for their health and living standards. The facts that now-prosperous Japan started as a low-wage producer, and that economic development cannot be achieved overnight, don't seem to register.

Nor does the fact that the allegedly exploited workers are often better off than their countrymen who remain in primitive agricultural or handicraft industries. An executive of one small company that manufactures plastic coat hangers in China told me that the wages he pays, which now average $25 per month, have made his workers the richest people in their villages. And Nike vice president David Taylor says that his company's subcontractors pay wages higher than the prescribed minima, plus bonuses for attendance, and provide free meals and medical care. He also points to an independent audit showing that 60 percent of the line workers in one Indonesian factory making Nike shoes save more than 25 percent of their monthly pay. Whether all those who work directly or indirectly for American firms do as well we do not know with certainty. But that seems to be the case in Central America: *Business Week* reports that Honduran workers who sew Levi's Dockers and Nike shorts average about $5.40 per day, twice the minimum wage.

The allegedly exploited workers are often better off than their countrymen who remain in primitive agricultural or handicraft industries.

The onslaught against the use of overseas workers has come at a particularly inauspicious time for the business community, which isn't in a very good position to fight back these days. True, the huge capital gains average shareholders have been earning have disposed them to be less critical of the performance of big corporations than would otherwise be the case, on the general theory that it is impolite to bite the hand that is enriching you. But those gains appear to be coming to an end. Watch for the row over executive compensation to flare up again when critics of Bob Dole's tax-cut plan point out that it is likely to favor high earners. Ross Perot is on the loose again, with federal funds that can be used to publicize the "big sucking sound" he hears in his head. And the newly popular notion that corporations should behave "responsibly," on behalf of all their "stakeholders," rather than merely maximize profits, can easily be expanded to include an obligation to go beyond the requirements of host-country laws in remunerating workers.

So self-styled protectors of the Honduran and Indonesian poor, egged on by the trade unions, will have fertile ground in which to sow their criticism of the callousness of corporate America. And executives will have no reservoir of goodwill on which to draw in their defense of the way they do business overseas. This, despite the fact that their businesses are providing work for virtually all who want it, at rising real-compensation levels, and without raising the prices consumers must pay for most of the goods they buy.

11

International Partnerships Must Reduce the Use of Child Labor

Navin Narayan

Navin Narayan is a staff writer for the Harvard International Review.

Child labor is both a cause of and a symptom of poverty in many nations. However, addressing the problem of child labor will require more than recognizing its connection to poverty. The world must acknowledge child labor as a violation of fundamental human rights because it severely damages the health of children, places children in abusive situations, and impedes the social and cultural progress of developing nations. Governments, human rights organizations, labor leaders, corporations, and health professionals must all work together to find effective ways to ensure that the world's children are educated and not exploited in jobs in multinational or illegal industries.

Two hours before New Delhi awakes, small girls are already toiling at their looms. Their nimble fingers tie delicate knots into what will one day become intricate and expensive rugs. Their master overlooks rows of cramped five- and six-year-old girls, and beats them if they talk or giggle. He feeds them only twice in their 18-hour workdays because if they overeat, the girls will slumber and be less productive. The girls, squinting their eyes to discriminate between the fine threads, hardly realize their progressive loss of vision—one of many adverse health effects of their grueling work. For all their intense work, they earn a pittance; nevertheless, it is a small but essential contribution to their families' funds. These girls are some of the world's youngest workers wrapped up in a complex form of exploitation known as child labor.

Child labor as an omnipresent social ill knows no boundaries. While children in India weave intricate rugs, children in Cambodia cut heavy bricks, often severing fingers or hands in the process. Other children working in Colombian and South African mines endure physiological de-

Reprinted from Navin Narayan, "Stolen Childhoods: Tackling the Health Burdens of Child Labor," *Harvard International Review*, Fall 1997, by permission of the *Harvard International Review*.

fects from heaving stones on their fragile backs. Child labor is not solely endemic to the developing world; over one million children are scattered across the valleys of California where they harvest crops in fields bathed with toxic pesticides.

Across the globe, more than 73 million children under the age of 15 work. One in every four children works in the developing world, yet these estimates do not capture the full breadth of child labor. Conventional statistics fail to account for children in hidden industries such as domestic work or in illegitimate industries such as drug trafficking. These numerous forms of child labor cripple the health of children and the well-being of the societies to which they belong. Especially in its most perverse form, child labor is a manifestation of poverty. Families cannot survive unless children supplement their parents' incomes with their meager contributions. However, the availability of child labor as a cheap alternative to adult labor displaces older workers and actually perpetuates poverty. Furthermore, children trapped in child labor fail to obtain the education necessary to attain higher-paying jobs once they become adults. While it is true that some forms of child labor such as after school work in non-hazardous industries develop a child's sense of familial responsibility and do not interfere with their education, in many industries, especially in poverty-stricken nations, child labor becomes an alternative to schooling rather than a supplement.

To treat child labor as a symptom of poverty, however, makes its eradication seem impossible. The concept of poverty is vague and does not offer a systematic approach to combating child labor. Instead, the world must understand child labor as a violation of children's most fundamental rights. These widely ratified rights offer a systematic approach to exposing child labor and tackling its brutal health effects.

Health burdens

The debilitating health effects of child labor cannot be overemphasized. Many forms of child labor thrust children into jobs that are as unsafe for children as they are for adults. Child sex workers in Thailand and Nepal, like their older counterparts, contract infectious diseases and struggle with psychological trauma. In other occupations, however, children are even more susceptible to disease and injury than their adult counterparts. Specific examples reveal the unique and horrific health burdens suffered by child laborers.

Children can be found in mining and quarrying occupations across Asia, Southern Africa, and Latin America. These children, working in congested and dusty environments, lug heavy stones on their shoulders and backs. With their bones and muscles not fully developed, the children suffer from bone brittling and other structural defects not usually encountered in adults. Mining and quarrying also stymie normal physical development by stunting the stature of children by as much as four centimeters. Additionally, child miners breathe in large quantities of silica dust. The silica forms patches along the sides of the lungs resulting eventually in silicosis, a breathing disorder which reduces the lung's vital capacity. Bronchitis, asthma, and pneumoconiosis are other frequently encountered breathing difficulties faced by miners and quarriers. Boys between the ages of 13 and 17, when the lungs undergo their most rapid growth, are especially susceptible to silicosis and fibrosis. Furthermore, the latency period for the disease, or the period between first exposure to silica and the onset of silicosis, is shorter for children than for adults.

The agricultural sector is the largest and most dangerous employer of children worldwide. Children harvest fruits and vegetables, climb ladders to prune orchards, care for farm animals, and drive large tractors. In the United States alone, 300 children and adolescents die each year from farm injuries while another 23,500 suffer from non-fatal trauma. Tractor fatalities alone account for more than half of all agricultural deaths each year. These injuries draw special attention to the ergonomic limitations faced by child laborers. Children are not physiologically developed enough to steer equipment designed for adults, such as tractors, combines, and forklifts. Furthermore, children, with shorter attention spans, are more likely to dangerously misuse such machinery.

Numerous forms of child labor cripple the health of children and the well-being of the societies to which they belong.

The agricultural sector also threatens the health of young harvesters who wade through fields and orchards sprayed with pesticides. Children, with thinner epidermal and dermal linings, are particularly susceptible to the toxic effects of pesticide poisonings. Child harvesters exposed to the organophosphate compounds of pesticides experience, as a group, higher rates of leukemia and other forms of cancer. Moreover, the proximity of children's living quarters to crops renders them vulnerable to pesticide drift during the spraying season. Working from daybreak to sundown in extreme temperatures, these children also experience fatigue and suffer from psychological depression. The psychological effects of child labor are especially striking in Sri Lanka where children revert to any escape available from their arduous work. Eager for sympathy and relief, the children swallow small amounts of pesticide in an attempt to become ill; instead they suffer often fatal consequences.

The garment industry, from Bangladesh's clothing factories to New York's sweatshops, also envelops millions of child laborers each year. While some children mix carcinogenic dyes, others weave fine dresses and saris. The industrial environment is dark, cramped, and deafening. Children exposed to dyes, formaldehyde, and industrial radiation later suffer from thyroid and other forms of cancer. With no ergonomic protection for their ears, children lose their hearing, and those handling scarcely visible threads suffer from gradual visual impairment. Furthermore, cardiovascular stress threatens children working in fiber factories more than their adult counterparts.

To exacerbate matters, the above ailments do not include the consistent physical beatings children endure from their masters for "indolence" or natural childlike behavior. Indeed, the true cost of many of the world's finest garments includes the deteriorating health of a child.

In addition to these overt forms of child exploitation, other forms of child labor exist where the health hazards are less obvious. For instance, the pumping of gasoline by minors exposes them to benzene which the scientific community has recently discovered to be a carcinogenic solvent promoting leukemia. In other industries, children do not work for an employer but rather work directly to support their own existence. With the will to survive, street children in developing countries scavenge through waste dumps in search of food or recyclable items. Boys and girls in parts of India diligently sort through hazardous hospital wastes in a quest for rags or cloths to vend. The occurrence of scabies, tetanus, septic boils and Hepatitis B is not uncommon among these children who often step over or dig through syringes and other infectious waste.

Other equally debilitating forms of employment evade traditional statistical measures of the child labor problem. Domestic work, for example, incarcerates many young girls in new homes away from their families. In one form of labor known as debt bondage, these girls, who are often beaten and sexually abused, receive no recompense for their work. Instead their labor merely pays back a debt loan owed by their parents to their new masters. The mistreated girls frequently suffer psychosocial disorders such as premature aging and depression. Indeed, the health burdens borne by the world's working children, with their childhoods stolen, highlight the true gravity of the child labor problem.

Children's rights

Respect for the fundamental rights of children is the very barometer of a society's well-being and future potential. Universally recognized children's rights also provide an effective means of combating child labor and jettisoning its intrinsic health burdens. The formal recognition of the rights of children stems back to 1919 with the adoption of the Minimum Age Convention No. 5 at the first session of the Geneva-based International Labor Organization (ILO). Following the session, 72 nations ratified the Convention, which established 14 years as the minimum age for children to be employed in industry. This first international effort to regulate the participation of children in industry was followed by a number of successive ILO conventions. In 1973, the ILO convention established fifteen as the minimum age of employment in the economic sector and has been ratified by close to 50 nations.

Seventy years after the first ILO convention in 1919, the United Nations General Assembly adopted the 1989 Convention on the Rights of the Child. The Convention singly enshrines the full range of civil political, economic, social, and cultural rights of children necessary to their survival, development, and protection in society. Because of the connection between child rights and survival and development, virtually all of the Convention's articles apply to the distressing effects of child labor. The articles address child labor-related areas ranging from education to health, nutrition, rest, and relaxation. In particular, Article 32 recognizes the right of children to be protected from work that threatens their health, education, or moral development. The Article further requires states to set minimum ages for employment and to regulate the working conditions of children. Article 24 more explicitly recognizes the right of children to enjoy the highest standards of health, while Article 28 details the expectation that all children receive a compulsory and free primary education.

Since its adoption, 173 countries—all countries except the Cook Islands, Oman, Somalia, Switzerland, the United Arab Emirates, and the United States—have ratified the Convention, making it the most widely ratified human rights treaty in history. Upon ratifying the treaty, the country is obliged to take all measures to fulfill its responsibility and obligation to children under the Convention. Thus, 96 percent of the world's children today live in states bound to uphold and protect the rights of children. This almost universally ratified human rights framework thus provides a consistent paradigm and solid foundation for tackling child labor.

Tackling child labor

The social purgation of child labor requires the united efforts of governments, non-governmental organizations (NGOs), health professionals, families, and child labor industries to uphold the fundamental rights of children. Governments must work to incorporate the principles of the Convention on the Rights of the Child and relevant ILO conventions into their legal frameworks. Wider child labor legislation consistent with the spirit of these conventions will more explicitly inscribe the illegality of child labor. Governments must also takes steps toward enforcing child labor legislation starting with the immediate elimination of the most hazardous forms of child labor.

Merely criminalizing child labor, however, does not tackle the full extent of the child labor problem. Governments must also uphold children's basic right to education. Without widely established primary schools, children will have no alternative but to return to the work force, where they will resume positions of subordination and exploitation. Provisions for primary education are especially necessary in rural areas, where the majority of the world's child laborers toil in the agricultural sector. Equipping children with basic education not only places them into higher paying jobs later but also deals a blow to the self-perpetuating cycle of child labor and poverty.

The world must understand child labor as a violation of children's most fundamental rights.

Additionally, governments must cooperate with health care workers to register all children at birth as called for by Article 7 of the Convention on the Rights of the Child. Registration will first provide labor inspectors and employers with every child's age so that they can accurately assess which individuals are old enough to work in any given industry. Registration also allows children access to education, health care, and other services to which they are entitled. Proper registration will also allow NGOs, health professionals, and governments to better gather and analyze data on child labor.

NGOs play a vital role in the elimination of child labor. As the watchdogs of government activity, NGOs must continue to expose the gaps where child labor thrives vibrantly and where employers and governments continue to trample over the rights of children. By portraying the bleak situation of children globally, NGOs increase the awareness of the child labor dilemma and draw in more anti-child labor activists. With the aid of modern technology and communication, NGOs may work through the media and take other measures to expose governments and industries that continue to promote or condone child labor.

The Rugmark campaign illustrates how NGOs successfully curtailed the incidence of child labor in the rug and carpet industry by mustering public pressure against the industry. In 1989, a number of grassroots NGOs across India, appalled at the more than 420,000 children toiling on looms, organized to form the South Asian Coalition on Child Servitude (SACCS). With the aid of the United Nations International Children's Fund (UNICEF) and other international organizations, SACCS launched the Rugmark campaign. The Rugmark label picturing a smiling face on a carpet promotes rugs made free of child labor. The Rugmark foundation awards licenses to use its "smiling carpet" logo only to manufacturers who submit to surprise inspections of their factories and looms. The international publicizing of the Rugmark campaign by NGOs has stymied the export of rugs lacking the Rugmark logo, while boosting sales of rugs with the label. With increased public awareness of child labor in the carpet industry, a number of carpet manufacturers have dropped their child employment practices to obtain the reputable Rugmark license.

Child labor is a complex social phenomenon connected to poverty, social values, and cultural circumstances which can only be eradicated through wide partnerships throughout society.

National and international corporations also bear responsibility to eradicate child employment. Specifically, the plight of child laborers demands that these corporations adopt codes of conduct that explicitly guarantee that neither they nor their subcontractors will violate the rights of children by engaging in illegal child labor. Corporations must further monitor their subcontractors for the presence of child employment, especially in child labor-ridden areas such as the textile industry.

International governments may also pressure each other to uphold the rights of children and abolish child labor. Governments have commonly used trade sanctions against nations employing children, believing that this practice would revolutionize labor practices and resolve the child labor problem. However, sanctions only affect export industries which exploit merely five percent of all child laborers. In some instances sanctions cause more harm than good.

The Harkin Bill, introduced by the United States Congress in 1992, is a case in point. The Harkin Bill, with the praiseworthy goal of prohibiting imports of products made by children under 15, threatened Bangladesh's garment industry. Before the bill even made the statute books, the industry began dismissing child workers from its factories. The displaced girls, however, without educational opportunities, turned to more hazardous jobs in unsafe workshops or to prostitution. The clear lesson from the Harkin Bill is that no single approach can effectively combat child labor. Displacing child labor without establishing educational facilities will only drive children to more "invisible" forms of employment. Furthermore, the Harkin example suggests that child labor opponents should conduct child-impact assessments before implementing any course of action.

Indeed, child labor is a complex social phenomenon connected to poverty, social values, and cultural circumstances which can only be eradicated through wide partnerships throughout society. Despite their complex roots, the Convention on the Rights of the Child and other ILO conventions offer a universal and easily understood mechanism for fighting child labor and for eliminating its crippling health effects. To uphold children's basic rights, governments, NGOs, health professionals, and industries must shift children from employment to education. The fight against child labor is a slow and arduous process. But what child would not opt for a brighter classroom over an ill-lit loom.

12

Campaigns Against Child Labor Are Protectionist and Imperialist

Llewellyn H. Rockwell

Llewellyn H. Rockwell is president of the Ludwig von Mises Institute in Auburn, Alabama. He is also editor of the Rothbard-Rockwell Report, *a monthly digest published by the Center for Libertarian Studies in Burlingame, California.*

Campaigns against child labor are an attempt on the part of unions and labor activists to protect American jobs by banning imports made by children in foreign factories. These protectionists, whose arguments have been bolstered by the left-wing emphasis on children's rights, concoct grim tales about the so-called exploitation of child laborers in the third world. Their true goal is not to help working children but to weaken the competition from foreign industries and to increase the power of unions in the U.S. labor market. Moreover, the attempt to impose first world labor standards on third world countries is a form of liberal cultural imperialism. If the anti-child-labor campaign succeeds, American consumers and manufacturers will face diminished access to inexpensive imports. A successful campaign against child labor would also drive working children out of their jobs and into increased poverty and hardship.

S hould we ban Third World imports because they were made by young girls working long hours in hot factories? The question itself is fraudulent, tailored to whip up public hysteria, bolster the moral standing of unions and restrict products rightly beloved by American consumers.

The unions are campaigning against retailers that import inexpensive goods from other countries. Unions and their congressional mouthpieces insist that products be labeled with a Labor Department sticker proclaiming: "No Sweat." That's supposed to mean it wasn't made in a sweatshop, although the slogan more aptly would be applied to the Labor Department, where a horde of bureaucrats live the life of Riley at taxpayer expense.

Of course, the tales about foreign sweatshops are part of a well-funded disinformation campaign that seeks to restrict the ability of American consumers to buy good products at reasonable prices. Thus, the specter of foreign child labor is merely excuse No. 1,345, or thereabouts, for why the U.S. government should run a mercantilistic trade policy. When the goal is to diminish foreign competition, secure union privilege and harm U.S. manufacturers and consumers who like imported products, any excuse—and any lie—will do.

For example, protectionists blab endlessly about infant industries, aging industries, trade imbalances, foreign dumping, intellectual-property rights, national defense, national sovereignty, overseas wages, racial pride, terrorism, defective products, the need for government revenue, the need to retaliate, dangerous avocados, killer tomatoes and now, at last, child labor.

Because of the length of their laundry list, protectionist arguments can be difficult to beat back. They don't have one good reason to restrict or forbid foreign imports, so they spew out new excuses as fast as the old ones are exposed as fakeries. Even better, they toss out 10 or 20 reasons in quick succession and hope that emotion will win out over economic sanity.

Thus the child-labor plea for protectionism is timed to ride the coattails of the new left-wing emphasis on children's rights, as exemplified by the Children's Defense Fund and Hillary Clinton's awful book. Sadly, it may work.

A left-wing demand

But the abolition of child labor long has been a left-wing demand. In 1896, the International Socialist and Trade Union Congress wanted to outlaw any work in any country by anyone under 16. As one old-line Communist put it: "Society may ask for cheap products" but "goods that have in them the flesh and blood of the future mothers of the toiling masses are not cheap." Such rhetoric employed against plain old industriousness, then and now, masks the real object: to keep out foreign goods and reduce the numbers of nonunion workers.

Notice that child-labor laws in this country are enforced not by the Department of Health and Human Services, but by the Department of Labor, which really should be called the Department of Labor Unions. The point of antichild-labor enforcement is to boot people out of the workforce where they compete with union labor and into public schools where they can be held hostage for 12 solid years of learning little but government propaganda.

Remember, when we talk about child labor at home or abroad, we are not talking about "children", but youth under 16. These young people are productive workers, which is precisely why labor unions feel so threatened by them. Why should they be denied the right to work and the right to contribute to family income?

Youth workers compete with overpaid union members for jobs and thereby bid wages down to a market level. In this sense, there is a direct analogy between campaigns against child labor and campaigns to increase the minimum wage. Both are supported by unions to make it too costly or downright impossible to employ younger, inexperienced workers who will work for less.

Child-labor laws came to Britain in the 19th century, thanks to propaganda from socialists and unions. In this country, all ages worked throughout that century without restriction from the government. But by the turn of the century, meat-packing unions succeeded in getting antichild-labor legislation and compulsory school-attendance laws passed in state after state.

One of the earliest campaigns against child labor concerned the employment of girls under 16 in American textile mills. The complaint was not that they were working but that they were willing to work for such low wages. The "girls who labored" in these factories, wrote a labor-allied economist, "cannot provide for their wants with the wages they earn." But, of course, it makes no sense—except to union workers—to solve the supposed problem of low wages by making it illegal for people to work.

I'm reminded of periodic campaigns against child labor by [former] Labor Secretary Robert Reich (and Elizabeth Dole before him). Invariably, the crimes involve hamburger joints allowing teenagers to work more hours per week than allowed by the department. But by restricting the hours they can work, the government denies valuable job experience to young people.

If you believed the Labor Department, you would think that child labor is a serious problem in the United States too. But it is far better that young people be given some chance of gaining income and valuable experience than entering the workforce after high school with neither skills nor the mental discipline to make them employable.

Labor protectionists can dream up endless stories of tiny babes slaving dawn to dusk for Third World moguls. We have no way to assess the truth of these tales, and the wise listener will consider the source. For workers to be valuable to employers, after all, they must be able to produce valuable work. If they are of an age to do so, who is to say that governments should intervene to prevent it?

Yet there is a deeper point. A high standard of living often is taken for granted in an industrial society. Among the marks of prosperity is the parental ability to delay the entry of their children into the workforce for many years.

Such an option is not available in poor countries. It takes time and capital accumulation to enable children to stay out of the workforce until late in their teen years. Meanwhile, the opportunity for people to work at all ages is a blessing, not a curse. To seek to deny work to people in other countries is not compassion, but merely leftist cultural imperialism.

Child labor is necessary

Child labor is a necessary part of economic development. Moreover, the presence of "sweatshops" suggests that some effort is being made to move beyond the hunter-gatherer status into the modern world. How ironic that the very people who moan about unemployment would favor laws making it illegal for an entire segment of the population to work.

In some poor countries, children are seen as liabilities or as mere consumable goods. The opportunity to put them to work in their early teens changes that and allows families undergoing extreme hardship to support themselves. Children contribute to family income and gain valuable experience and are seen as a net asset to families and society.

But when children are not allowed to work, their economic value to families is reduced and they become net liabilities. The enforcement of antichild-labor laws thereby reduces the incentive to bear children while raising the incentives to abort. If you care about the status of children in the Third World, the repeal of child-labor laws should be a top priority.

Consider the high-profile case of 15-year-old Wendy Diaz, the Honduran factory worker who is the unions' present poster child. In her story, she worked for Global Fashions at the age of 13—and, like most people, claims to have been underpaid and overworked. As she admits, however, she did this voluntarily to support her three younger brothers.

Tales about foreign sweatshops are part of a . . . disinformation campaign that seeks to restrict the ability of American consumers to buy good products at reasonable prices.

The relevant question is: How would Wendy Diaz and her brothers be better off if she had no job and the factory had no American market for its products? More than likely, she and her younger brothers would go hungry. If American unions succeed in cutting off trade, shouldn't they be held accountable for such a tragedy? And why isn't it child labor when American unions employ this poor kid in their political campaign?

If unions really were concerned for the welfare of children, they would favor more foreign trade, not less. The consequences of boycotts for Latin-American and Asian countries (and notice that the countries chosen for attack are the ones that export goods also produced by unions) will be to make everyone in those countries worse off, not to speak of American consumers. Industries that rely on labor of all kinds will go under, and opportunities for families to lift themselves out of poverty will be stamped out.

Boycotts of products from these countries also strengthen their governments at the expense of the market. The informal and underground sectors in which youths are employed are anxious to avoid detection and not only because of the diverse age of their workforce. A government crackdown on child labor not only will deny job opportunities to people; it will mandate compliance with all sorts of outrageous taxes and regulations.

The truth is that child labor is a common practice in every country in the world, including the First World, but most especially in the developing world—and thank goodness. It occurs despite the fact that virtually every country has laws on its books preventing child labor. To get around the laws, capitalists and entrepreneurs, including family businessmen, must engage in heroic acts of defiance of the ruling regime.

There are only three groups pushing for more restrictions on imports: domestic producers who seek special immunity from competition, labor unions that want consumers to be taxed to prop up their inflated wages, and the federal government which seeks ever more power over economic life. This cabal has conspired for decades to rip off the American consumer using fraudulent economics and made-up scenarios of foreign duplicity.

Child labor is only the most recent excuse. It, too, should be dismissed out of hand, and the perpetrators of the public-relations blitz denounced as charlatans. It's not foreign capitalists who are abusing children, but American labor unions and their wholly owned politicians.

13

Workplace Codes Could Prevent Sweatshop Abuses

Michael Posner and Lynda Clarizio

Michael Posner is the executive director of the Lawyers Committee for Human Rights. Lynda Clarizio is a founding member of the Washington Advisory Council for the Lawyers Committee for Human Rights.

Initiated by Bill Clinton, the Apparel Industry Partnership is a coalition of apparel companies, human rights organizations, advocacy groups, and unions that is working to end the use of sweatshop labor. This coalition has created a Workplace Code of Conduct that requires participating companies and manufacturers to provide humane working conditions. The Code, which will be enforced by inspectors and independent monitors, prohibits the use of child labor and forced labor and ensures that employees work in safe, abuse-free environments. The Code also guarantees workers the right to collective bargaining and a minimum standard on wages and benefits. If more companies join the Apparel Industry Partnership, the effort to eradicate child labor and sweatshops will be successful.

Since 1996, we have been part of a unique coalition of apparel companies, unions, and advocacy groups, all brought together by President Bill Clinton in a groundbreaking effort to end sweatshop conditions in the manufacture of clothing and footwear around the world.

The Apparel Industry Partnership

In its first eight months of deliberations, this effort, called the Apparel Industry Partnership, succeeded in developing an industrywide Workplace Code of Conduct addressing such issues as child labor, forced labor, workplace discrimination, and compulsory hours of work. It has also proposed internal and external monitoring principles for companies that embrace the Code. A third essential accomplishment of the Partnership is a commitment to create an independent association, including both apparel

Reprinted from Michael Posner and Lynda Clarizio, "An Unprecedented Step in the Effort to End Sweatshops," *Human Rights*, Fall 1997, by permission of the American Bar Association. Copyright © American Bar Association.

companies and human rights groups, to oversee compliance with the Code and set qualifications for external factory monitors.

This is a precedent-setting agreement in an industry where there have been wholesale violations of human rights. Sweatshop practices remain commonplace in the United States, despite laws and an extensive government regulatory system. In other parts of the world, places like Haiti, China, Guatemala, and India, local laws protecting workers are weak, enforcement weaker still. Efforts at enforcement are complicated by the structure of the apparel industry, where products made abroad are typically produced by contractors, subcontractors, and suppliers, not in company-owned factories.

The media have reported on young children in the apparel industry living and working in slave-like conditions, on grossly unsafe working conditions, and on workers forced to work unreasonably long hours for meager pay. A flurry of such reports occurred in 1996 when it was revealed that some of Wal-Mart's line of Kathie Lee Gifford sportswear—in which the TV personality was receiving $5 million for the use of her name—was being made by 13-year-old girls in Honduras working 20-hour days for 31 cents an hour.

Reacting to these reports and a growing public outrage, President Clinton convened the Apparel Industry Partnership at the White House in August 1996. Liz Claiborne, NIKE, Phillips–Van Heusen, and L.L. Bean were among the companies that attended. Also invited were labor unions and human rights, religious, and consumer organizations. At the president's urging, and with steady prodding from the Labor Department, our diverse and often contentious coalition has hammered out a series of interim agreements that together represent a significant and practical first step in the effort to eradicate sweatshops.

Serious about human rights law

We were at first skeptical about the sincerity and seriousness of the effort. Was it merely a public relations ploy? The Partnership, after all, was and remains an informal private initiative, not a federal advisory commission. We had no money, no staff, no legal authority. As our monthly meetings progressed, though, it became clear that most of the participating companies were seriously asking about their obligations under human rights law, and were prepared to make some important commitments. On the other side, the human rights, religious, consumer, and labor groups recognized that the Partnership presented a unique opportunity to urge reforms and to effect substantial change in a troubled and largely unregulated industry.

The first order of business for the Partnership was to devise a Workplace Code of Conduct defining decent and humane working conditions and intended to apply to the factories of participating companies as well as their contractors all over the world. By the spring of 1997, members of the Partnership had reached agreement on nine essential issues elements of the Code. They are: prohibitions on forced labor, on child labor, and on harassment and abuse; protections governing nondiscrimination, health and safety, and freedom of association and collective bargaining; and minimum standards for wages and benefits, hours of work, and overtime compensation.

Each of these issues generated spirited debate. On child labor, for instance, some argued that no one under 15 should miss school by working, but others pointed out that some countries allow the employment of 14-year-olds. In the end, an exception was made for countries where this lower age is permitted. On wages and benefits, advocacy groups pressed strongly for a living wage, not merely one that meets the local legal minimum. On this critical issue, compromise language was adopted, which sets a standard requiring payment of either the local minimum wage or the prevailing industry wage, whichever is higher. It also contains an acknowledgment that "Employers recognize that wages are essential to meeting employees' basic needs."

Our . . . coalition has hammered out a series of interim agreements that together represent a significant and practical first step in the effort to eradicate sweatshops.

While many companies have adopted codes of conduct aimed at protecting their workers, the Code of the Apparel Industry Partnership is unprecedented because it is intended to be an industrywide minimum standard. Even more important, however, are the enforcement mechanisms that the Partnership is working to develop to ensure compliance with the Code.

Currently, only a small minority of apparel companies use outside monitors to ensure that their codes are being followed. The Partnership has proposed that companies desiring to adhere to the Code must conduct inspections of their factories and those of their contractors in accordance with specific monitoring principles and must agree to open up these factories to inspections by independent external monitors. The new association would ensure compliance with the Code by establishing criteria and developing procedures for the qualification of external monitors, designing audit and other instruments for the establishment of baseline monitoring practices, and serving as a source of information to consumers about companies that are found to be in compliance with the Code. The association would include labor unions and human rights, consumer, and religious groups as well as industry members.

Current status of the negotiations

For companies, of course, a vital reason for participating in the Partnership and joining the new association is the prospect of being able to demonstrate to consumers that they are taking credible steps to end sweatshop practices. Of the 10 original industry members of the Partnership, NIKE, Reebok, Liz Claiborne, Phillips–Van Heusen, L.L. Bean, Tweeds, Nicole Miller, and Patagonia still belong and appear likely to be founding members of the association. The advocacy groups in the Partnership include the Lawyers Committee for Human Rights, UNITE (Union of Needletrades, Industrial and Textile Employees), the International Labor Rights Fund, the National Consumers League, the Robert F. Kennedy Memorial Center, the Retail, Wholesale and Department Store Union, and the Interfaith Center on Corporate Responsibility. The Partnership continues to meet monthly to develop the structure of the new association and the accreditation of external monitors.

Though the companies in the Partnership include many of the leaders in the field, they do not by themselves dominate the industry. For this process to succeed, a larger percentage of the industry must be willing to join this effort to create an objective, verifiable process to ensure that products are made without exploitative labor.

14

Workplace Codes Will Not Prevent Sweatshop Abuses

Medea Benjamin

Medea Benjamin is the director of Global Exchange, a San Francisco–based human rights organization.

Some U.S. companies that sell goods produced in foreign factories have agreed to adopt the Workplace Code of Conduct—a list of minimum standards for treatment of factory workers that was drawn up by a coalition of industry, labor, and human rights groups. These minimum standards will not adequately protect workers' human rights because they do not guarantee a living wage, freedom from mandatory overtime, or the right to collective bargaining. Eradicating the use of sweatshops will require continued public pressure on abusive corporations to treat workers with respect.

With much fanfare at a Rose Garden ceremony, President Clinton announced that a coalition of industry, human rights and labor groups had reached a breakthrough agreement to end sweatshops. Saying that the lives of factory workers are as important as the fabric they make, President Clinton called the agreement a historic step that will "give American consumers greater confidence in the products they buy." Companies that voluntarily adhere to this new code will be able to tag their products "sweatshop free."

But before consumers go on a guilt-free shopping spree, they should take a moment to look at some of the details of this agreement.

A breakthrough agreement?

• *Companies shall pay the prevailing minimum wage or industry wage.* Companies are flocking to countries that deliberately set the minimum wage below subsistence to attract foreign investment. In Vietnam, Nike pays 20 cents an hour; in Haiti, Disney pays 30 cents an hour. These wages, while the legal minimum, are not enough to buy three decent meals a day, let

Reprinted from Medea Benjamin, "No Sweat for Companies to Agree," *Los Angeles Times*, editorial, April 17, 1997, by permission of the author.

alone pay for transportation, housing, clothing and health care. U.S. companies should pay wages that allow workers to live healthy, dignified lives. They should swiftly and publicly commit themselves to paying at least double the legal minimum in their overseas factories. And they should agree to pay restitution to workers who have been cheated out of past wages.

• *Except in extraordinary business circumstances, employees shall not be required to work more than 60 hours a week.* In addition to accepting a 60-hour week as the norm—which in itself is outrageous—the agreement provides no guidelines on what constitutes "extraordinary circumstances." Moreover, it only addresses "mandatory" overtime. Already, apparel factory workers put in endless "voluntary" overtime. There should be no mandatory overtime and if workers were paid a living wage for an eight-hour day, excessive "voluntary" overtime would cease.

We cannot leave the fate of the world's apparel workers in the hands of presidential commissions.

• *Employees shall be compensated for overtime hours at the legal rate, or where none exists, at a rate at least equal to their regular hourly compensation rate.* Labor unions the world over call for overtime to be paid at a higher rate than the regular hourly wage. The agreement should call for at least time-and-a-half pay for overtime.

• *Employers shall recognize and respect the right of employees to freedom of association and collective bargaining.* Recognition of these rights is certainly a positive step. Unfortunately, many U.S. companies choose to work in countries or free-trade zones where independent organizing is illegal and where workers who stand up for their rights are severely repressed. To give this recognition of workers' rights meaning, U.S. companies must pressure local governments to allow workers the freedom to organize, call for the release of all those jailed for their organizing efforts and require companies to rehire in their own factories workers who have been fired for organizing.

• *Companies shall utilize independent external monitors to ensure that the [agreement] is implemented.* The agreement does not insist that companies use local human rights, labor or religious groups that have the trust of the workers and knowledge of local conditions. Instead, the companies can use private accounting firms and merely "consult regularly" with these local institutions. It is extremely unlikely that employees working under repressive conditions would speak openly to representatives of accounting firms. Meaningful monitoring must be conducted by respected not-for-profit entities.

More action is needed

According to this agreement, companies could still pay their workers 20 cents an hour, coerce them into countless hours of "voluntary overtime," use accounting firms that have no connection to workers as their external monitors and be rewarded for this behavior with a "no sweatshop" seal of approval.

The results of this task force's eight-month process demonstrate all too clearly that we cannot leave the fate of the world's apparel workers in the hands of presidential commissions. To really put an end to sweatshops, we must continue to mobilize public opinion, support struggling factory workers and pressure abusive corporations until workers at home and abroad are paid living wages and treated with dignity.

15

Product Labeling Programs May Not Reduce Child Labor

Julie V. Iovine

Julie V. Iovine is a writer for the New York Times *News Service.*

Several carpet importers and manufacturers have responded to governmental and consumer aversion to child labor by participating in programs intended to assure customers that their rugs were made without child labor. These programs use inspectors to monitor the production of rugs and affix labels to carpets made by participating manufacturers. Such tactics may be ineffective, however. Labeling programs often have too few inspectors to monitor an entire domain of carpet production, and it is possible that these inspectors are bribed to lie about the use of child labor. Furthermore, rug weaving is often a necessary family enterprise that contributes to the economy of developing nations. Rather than banning the use of child labor outright, consumers should support strategies that provide benefits for children.

Buyers of handmade imported rugs are used to petting the plush, appraising the pattern and checking the dimensions. But not until now have so many buyers been inspecting a rug's flip side, searching out a little tag that says the rug was made without child labor.

With the new ban on imports of goods made by children in bondage, signed by President Clinton in October 1997, it has become the latest must-have label.

"Our customers are really aware," said Kimberley Aylward, the spokeswoman for Garnet Hill, a mail-order catalogue that sells $1 million in imported rugs each year. "They want assurances even before they place an order that no kids were involved."

Accurate numbers do not exist for the number of children working in servitude in the making of rugs in South Asia, said Darlene Atkins, the public policy coordinator at the Child Labor Coalition in Washington. Estimates range from 300,000 to one million, the latter figure provided by the South Asian Coalition on Child Servitude. Most of the children working in the rug industry are in India and Pakistan, Ms. Atkins said.

Retailers market their awareness

Although Congress passed the new law, it did not appropriate any additional money for the Custom Service to monitor imports or track violators. Retailers and manufacturers in the imported carpet business, estimated at $1.3 billion a year, are aware of the risk to their image in selling items made by children and are looking for ways to market their awareness to concerned customers. These range from self-monitoring—Ikea and Pottery Barn are among the stores that hire agents to inspect looms periodically—to labeling programs, of debatable efficacy, that monitor production and use the fees they collect to set up schools.

Frank Hagemann, a policy analyst at the International Labor Organization in Geneva, said that the number of rug manufacturers signed up for programs worldwide is too small to measure. But "awareness is increasing rapidly," he said. Five years ago, he pointed out, there were no programs at all.

Right now, the most visible marketing tool is labeling. The international labor group says six labeling programs currently operate in India, Germany, Switzerland, Brazil and the United States. The two largest programs are Rugmark and Kaleen.

Rugmark, an international non-profit organization that has enlisted 145 manufacturers from India and Nepal, monitors production and uses fees paid to it to finance three schools in Nepal and India. Kaleen, which is promoted by the Government of India in collaboration with the carpet industry, requires that every exporter contribute 0.25 percent of the export price of each rug to the program and register every loom in return for the Kaleen label. The money raised is used for schools.

Passing laws and affixing labels may not be the best way to help exploited children.

Only the winsome, smiley-face Rugmark label certifies that products are made without child labor. "We guarantee to the public that we have done a thorough inspection," said Terrence Collingsworth, the general counsel to the International Labor Rights Fund in Washington and a member of the Rugmark board, adding, "if you want to sell rugs in the United States, you're going to need some kind of certificate."

Ike Timianko, the owner of the Central Carpet in Manhattan, said: "If I don't see a tag, I don't buy the rug. My customers want to know."

Is accurate monitoring possible?

But effective monitoring remains the biggest snag. Critics say that any retailer offering a blanket guarantee is being naïve—at best—given the workload of inspectors.

Rugmark, despite its $1 million budget, has only 18 inspectors who are supposed to make surprise visits to 18,636 looms. Kaleen turns the work of monitoring looms at 2,400 carpet export houses over to an independent Indian research organization with 18 inspectors.

"Labeling programs are futile," said Chris Walter, the project director at Cultural Survival, a nonprofit human-rights organization in Boston. "Labels can and will be bought."

Elliott Schrage, an adjunct professor at Columbia University's business school who has helped coordinate an effort by the sports equipment industry to stop using children to stitch soccer balls in Pakistan, says that passing laws and affixing labels may not be the best way to help exploited children. "Without a video camera on every loom in every home where rugs are made," he said, "there's no way you can know if children were involved."

Opportunities are abundant for inspectors to demand bribes in return for lying about the involvement of children.

James Tufenkian, an American rug manufacturer who employs some 6,000 weavers in Nepal and who is a board member at Rugmark, says that while Rugmark's heart is "100 percent in the right place, it's difficult to know what's really going on when production is so spread out in the weavers' homes."

Dan Hodges, the president of Pande Cameron & Company, a Manhattan importer of rugs from India, contends that all labeling programs are vulnerable to corruption. He said that opportunities are abundant for inspectors to demand bribes in return for lying about the involvement of children.

Ikea does not place any tags on its rugs because "we would have to have people out there all the time watching, and without that, we cannot make a real guarantee," said Marianne Barner, a manager at Ikea headquarters in Almhult, Sweden. She added that the Ikea chain pays another company to make random visits to looms.

At Pottery Barn, "our position is that child labor is an issue that we cannot afford to be associated with," said Patrick Connolly, a vice president. Some Kaleen rugs are evident in its stores, but he said, "Our goal is not to get a label on every rug but to make sure there has been no illegal use of children."

ABC Carpet and Home in Manhattan, with annual sales volumes of $60 million in rugs, has so far refused to affix any labels to the rugs they manufacture in South Asia. It employs 6 inspectors for 1,000 looms.

"The tags are a joke," says Graham Head, managing director at ABC. "The only ones profiting from them are the makers of the tags themselves."

The new law specifically bans imports by children in bondage, estimated at $100 million worth of goods each year, for the most part rugs and carpets. ABC claims that not enough of a distinction has been made between bonded, or indentured labor, which all agree is intolerable, and cottage labor, where a group of people, often related and perhaps including children, all contribute to piecework production. Ikea, for example, favors banning all children having any role in the making of the carpets they sell. Making a distinction between family work and bonded labor, said Ms. Barner, is too complicated. "We say 'No child, period,'" she said.

Mr. Head of ABC Carpet and many others say the impact of such blanket prohibitions go against the natural rhythms of rural-based economies and could be damaging if they don't offer children the all-important alternative of an education. "If you want to really tackle the problems of poor countries, don't take away one of the only forms of income they have," said Mr. Head.

Mr. Walter agrees. "Just not working doesn't solve anything," he said. "In a single family some of the children may be working so that others can go to school."

Referring to cottage industries, Mr. Walter and many observers are sensitive to the issues of Western values applied to foreign cultures. "I see it as an issue of cultural domination," said Carol Bier, curator of Eastern Hemisphere collections at the Textile Museum in Washington. "In many cultures the economies are very different from our own, many are family-based and the set-ups are very different from documentable child abuse. Rug weaving is one of the most perfect examples of a sustainable economy in developing countries. In Turkey virtually every living room will have a loom in it.

"There is pride and delight felt by the whole family with their rugs," she added, noting that a child well-versed in the art of weaving often has a highly sophisticated grasp of complicated mathematics. "To ban all that could have a devastating effect."

With time, the mounting concern of consumers may be seasoned with a commitment to programs that really help children. With cottage labor so important to the survival of developing economies, Mr. Hodges, the Manhattan rug importer, said, "I just hope the new ban leaves plenty of room for exceptions."

16

Youth Activism Can Help Reduce Child Labor

Craig Kielburger, interviewed by *Multinational Monitor*

Craig Kielburger, a high school student from Toronto, Canada, is the founder of Free the Children, a student-run initiative to end child labor. He is interviewed by Multinational Monitor, *a monthly journal that focuses on the issues of globalization, labor, the environment, and international trade.*

The activism of Free the Children, a youth-run organization that urges consumers to buy child-labor-free products, proves the effectiveness of young people's involvement in campaigns against the use of child labor. The organization's activities—which include investigations of sweatshop conditions, letter-writing campaigns to governments and corporations, and international petitions promoting education and children's rights—have successfully encouraged governments to take direct steps to eliminate the use of child labor.

Multinational Monitor: *How did you become involved in working on this issue?*

Craig Kielburger: [In 1995,] I read in the paper about the murder of Iqbal Masih, the Pakistani child labor activist. The fact that we were both the same age caught my attention right away. I read that at the age of four he was working 12 hours a day, six days a week at a carpet factory, and that by age 10 he began speaking out against child labor. I contrasted his life with mine and I thought if he could do so much, that I should try to do something too.

I began to read up on child labor, which I thought was eliminated. I thought it was basically a nineteenth century kind of thing that didn't exist anymore. I learned that about 200 million children work throughout the world. I started speaking about child labor at my school and eventually founded Free the Children, which is rapidly expanding and now has chapters in Canada, the United States and in Switzerland.

How were you exposed to the issue of child labor?

After Free the Children started, the International Program for the

Reprinted from "Free the Children: An Interview with Craig Kielburger," *Multinational Monitor,* January/February 1997, by permission of *Multinational Monitor.*

Elimination of Child Labor suggested that Free the Children send a delegation to a Third World country to investigate child labor practices. At the same time, a friend, Alam Rahman, who is a student at the University of Toronto and is of Bangladesh descent, was going to Bangladesh. It worked out that Alam, who speaks Banglai, and I went on a seven-week tour of five countries—Nepal, India, Pakistan, Thailand and Bangladesh. My parents paid for my trip.

I spoke to many children over there. You can read about child labor, but to really understand it, you have to look into their eyes and see where they are working. I went to a brick kiln where children made bricks all day. I tried it, just to see how hard it was. I only did it a little while and was exhausted. I couldn't imagine children working at this all day.

Horrible work environments

Under what conditions do they work?

Horrible. I met children with arthritis in their hands, children with their hands severely cut. One girl I met worked at a metals factory; she showed me her severely burned arms and legs, which happened when she spilled some hot metals on herself. I met another eight-year-old girl who worked in a recycling factory in India, separating syringes from used needles. No protective clothing whatsoever. She never heard of AIDS; wore no gloves or shoes. I saw her walk barefoot over needles strewn on the factory floor. After a while, my guide suddenly dragged me away. I couldn't understand why until he told me outside that another child worker there warned him that if the factory master saw this girl talking with me, he would beat her.

Child labor physically, morally, socially and intellectually stunts children.

I met two boys in India who worked in a carpet factory; Nageshwer, age 14 and Monhan, age nine. They both began work at the carpet factory at the age of seven. Nageshwer showed me scars all over his body—hands, arms, legs, and even on his throat where he was branded with a hot iron when he helped his younger brother and a friend escape from the bondage. But he was unsuccessful and was caught by the loom owner. This was a type of punishment for him. Because of the branding on his throat, he could not speak for several months. But his first words were a song about how not to give up hope for freedom.

Monhan told the story of two other young boys who tried to escape from the same factory. They were caught by the loom owner and beaten and knifed to death in front of all the other children who were forced to watch this as a symbol of what would happen to them if they tried to escape. The bodies were taken and thrown into a lake. After a raid on this factory was conducted freeing the children, the parents of the murdered boys asked where were their children. The loom owner simply said they had run away into the forest. He was never prosecuted for his crime.

Monhan, who was freed in the carpet raid, told me how he was beaten when he cried for his mother. So he spoke to his mother in dreams at night. And I had the opportunity to accompany some of these children back to their homes, and I saw Monhan finally meet and speak with his mother. And the one thing I think I will never forget was when we were driving down a road taking these children home, and our jeep got stuck halfway across a lake. Everyone just piled out of the jeep and started pushing the jeep. When we finally pushed it out of the lake, we were sopping wet. It was very cold and many of us has fallen into the water—and when we all piled back into the jeep, the children just started singing about how they were free and they were going home again.

How much are they paid?

At the brick kiln, child workers are paid 30 cents for every 100 bricks they make. Even that money doesn't go too far because they buy their food from the factory store.

Why children work

Why do they work?

In some cases parents send them to work off a debt when the parents need a loan.

In some cases, children are tricked into bondage. For example, there was a raid on a carpet factory while I was in Asia where 23 children were freed. They had been tricked into bondage by the loom owner who promised them a fair wage and safe working conditions. And they were promised that they would be taught a skill to help support themselves in the future. They ended up working 15 hours a day; from seven in the morning until ten at night—all for the equivalent of around 20 cents a day, which they were forced to exchange for one meal of rice.

Some people in developing countries say people in richer countries should not criticize child labor. They say people in richer countries do not understand the cultural context in which child labor takes place, and that rich countries permitted and relied on child labor in similar stages of development. How do you respond to these arguments?

I'm all for children taking on responsibilities, but I draw the line on exploitation and oppression of children. Child labor physically, morally, socially and intellectually stunts children.

The success has been . . . the number of young people who realize the power that they have and that they can take that power and bring about change.

What sort of products do child laborers make?

Because a company uses subcontracting, it is extremely difficult to know what products are made with child labor. In many cases, the companies do not even know. Perhaps the company doesn't want to know. If companies truly wanted to know, they could find out by putting clauses in their trading agreements and by basically checking the books—checking for things, like, so many people working so many hours, so many products produced. And then asking, is this feasible? Does this all work out? If not, then where are these extra products coming from? Perhaps something is behind it, maybe it is child labor. Also, the company can do a lot of surprise checks, where they come in and see the working conditions. So that when the company arrives they don't find a clean floor with a banner saying "welcome."

Taking action against child labor

It is unbelievable the long list of products made with child labor—from carpets to medical equipment. If you can tell that this particular carpet was made by children, then people can choose not to buy that product. That's why you need a label on each product saying no child labor was used making this product. I know of many products, but you can never tell which product is made by children. For example, one shoe may have been made with child labor and not another shoe. You can't tell. That's the difficulty and that's why a labeling system has to be introduced, so that consumers can have a choice.

But product labeling is not the only way we can take action against child labor. We also have to push for education, protection and the rights of the child. Although the labeling system has to come about, they will not affect children who work as domestics, children who do not produce products for export, children in agriculture, children who work on the streets and in the sex trades. All this also has to be addressed, as well.

If consumers in industrialized countries boycott those products, do they hurt the exporting countries which need foreign exchange?

Well, I don't think it necessarily hurts the countries. One thing that is argued is that it may hurt the child. What has to happen is when you pull the children out of the factory you have to replace them with the adults—the relatives of the children. These relatives can form trade unions and fight for better working conditions and higher wages. That's why factory owners want children—they are cheap! Quite often, having children working brings down adult wages. So, when you put the adult in they receive a higher wage than the child, and they can better support the family, and the child can go to school; breaking the cycle of poverty.

What kinds of activities have you undertaken to draw attention to the issue of child labor?

We've done letter writing campaigns and petitions to governments and businesses asking governments to live up to their promises that were made at the 1990 World Summit on Children. We are pressuring world leaders to make education and protection of children a priority. You have to address this internationally because you can no longer look at a single country because basically countries don't exist anymore. It's the world level you are looking at, and it's a global scale. This problem is a global problem.

How successful have your efforts been?

We actually feel we have been quite successful. Our Minister of External Affairs in Canada just passed a resolution which says that Canadians who go overseas and molest children—engage in prostitution with a child overseas—can be prosecuted under Canadian law. The Canadian government also has allocated $700,000 to the International Program for the Elimination of Child Labor. And the government is sending officials overseas, to Germany, to look at how Rugmark—the labeling system of carpets made without child labor—works and bring it into Canada. But, mainly the success has been the number of young people who are getting involved—the number of young people who realize the power that they have and that they can take that power and bring about change.

17

Educators Should Encourage Student Activism Against the Use of Sweatshops

Steven Friedman

Steven Friedman is a teacher at Brandeis Hillel Day School in California.

Teachers should not be afraid to encourage their students to protest against American companies that use sweatshop labor. Students are often invited to participate in moral or political causes—such as organizing food drives or serving meals to the homeless—so the promotion of student activism against the use of sweatshops should not be considered too controversial or politically biased. While educators should pursue a fair and balanced analysis of social issues in the classroom, they must also recognize that teaching is never politically neutral. Inviting students to take direct action against the use of sweatshops fosters the desire for social justice and political engagement that creates positive change in the world.

To protest or not to protest, that was the question.

After showing my seventh- and eighth-grade Judaic studies class *Mickey Mouse Goes to Haiti,* a 28-minute documentary about the exploitation of workers in factories contracted to Disney, I once again faced this dilemma.

By showing the video, produced by the National Labor Committee (NLC), I hoped to encourage some activism. But I was afraid of getting in trouble for influencing the students on what some would consider a political issue. Instead of boldly proposing direct action, I suggested the class write letters to Disney headquarters.

My student Lizzie Louis had another idea. She asked if we could organize a demonstration outside one of Disney's stores in San Francisco. I told her it was a great idea but that the school would never sanction such an activity. My parting words to her were, "Let me see if I can arrange something for after school."

I was stalling.

As the school's community service coordinator, I'd never shied away

Reprinted from Steven Friedman, "Taking Action Against Disney," *Rethinking Schools*, Summer 1997, by permission of the author.

from raising political or moral issues. Indeed, I'd helped my students get involved in a variety of important causes or projects: corresponding through art and letters with patients who have life-threatening illnesses (mostly cancer and AIDS); serving meals to the homeless; tutoring and mentoring children in one of the county's poorest neighborhoods; collecting food, toys and clothing for area shelters and food banks; volunteering at a prison day care center. So why was I reluctant about my students protesting against Disney?

Disney contracts with factories in Haiti, Honduras, Indonesia, Thailand, and China. Independent monitoring groups (sponsored by unions, religiously affiliated groups, or organizations in those countries) as well as American journalists have confirmed widespread abuses and horrendous working conditions at many of these factories. I knew I was on solid ground with respect to the extent of injustices in Disney's sweatshops. But I was still afraid.

Can educators be neutral?

My apprehension was partly because of a past experience. In 1996, my fifth-graders viewed NLC's first video, *Zoned for Slavery*, about the inhumane working conditions in Central American factories which make Disney products. Afterward, my fifth-graders and I wrote letters of protest to Disney CEO Michael Eisner. After tepid responses from one of his vice presidents, the students suggested we provide the school community with a list of which clothing manufacturers used sweatshop labor in countries such as Haiti and El Salvador. The students and I felt that if people knew which manufacturers relied on sweatshops, they might boycott these companies.

After I published the list of the guilty companies twice in the school's weekly newsletter, the school's director told me to stop. He said that by becoming a political activist, I was perilously close to muddying my role as a neutral educator.

The accusation was strange because I teach at a private Jewish school where we spend a significant portion of time learning about ethics and values and relating them to our lives. We go beyond teaching about Biblical precepts—such as the commandment to leave the corners of your field or portions of your harvest for the poor—and stress modern applications of these ancient laws, such as helping at soup kitchens or stocking food at local food banks.

But now I had been told that I had crossed a line.

I printed the list once more. The director then told me that my future community service columns would need his prior approval. Apparently it was okay to advertise clothing drives or ask for money to help an inner-city school purchase supplies, but it was "too political" and "too activist" to provide people with information about companies that routinely deny basic rights to workers, many of them children who labor for U.S. markets.

Why, I asked myself, is it too political to highlight the exploitation and repression of workers who earn 7 cents to sew a *101 Dalmatians* outfit that retails for $19.95? How can anyone remain neutral when workers, mostly teenage women, are forced to work 12–16 hours a day making Disney toys in dusty, sweltering factories using dangerous chemicals?

What the director failed to tell me, but what I knew, were the real reasons I'd been reprimanded. The school was afraid to offend board members who might own stock in Disney; it wanted to be able to attract donations without appearing too political or too controversial. In other words, we had to remain neutral to protect investments in Disney and to secure funding for the school.

The complexities of classroom activism

I realize there are complicated issues involved in trying to determine when and how it is appropriate for a teacher to guide student activism. For instance, teachers need to be sensitive to the importance of letting students discuss, analyze, and make up their own minds about social issues, rather than merely allowing them to regurgitate what they perceive to be the teacher's views. And, as is true with any field trip or out-of-classroom activity, communication with parents and parental permission is essential.

But the complexities of the issue should not be used to hide the reality that teaching is never politically neutral. Everything educators do or don't do can be classified as political. If it's okay to promote progressive behavior by students (food drives, meals to the homeless), why shouldn't we guide students into social activism against inhumane working conditions that help cause poverty and homelessness? And I doubt that a group of middle school students protesting against Disney is the revolutionary straw that will break the back of the empire.

I knew I had to answer Lizzie's question. When word leaked out that I might organize an action against Disney, more students in her class asked about helping and attending. Then the class studied a unit on hunger and poverty and connected the dire conditions of the poor in the Third World with the policies of U.S. corporations subsidized by the U.S. government. The issue of a protest resurfaced. Then some of my former fifth-grade letter-writing activists questioned me about pursuing the topic of sweatshop labor the following year (I do not teach the sixth-grade Judaica class). How could I dodge the issue any longer?

How can anyone remain neutral when workers, mostly teenage women, are forced to work 12–16 hours a day making Disney toys in dusty, sweltering factories using dangerous chemicals?

The answer came when the NLC announced an international week of action against Disney, Dec. 7-14, 1996. A gift had landed in my lap: the NLC was sponsoring the demonstration I'd been afraid to organize. All I had to do was invite my students to the rally on a non-school day and we'd have our opportunity to get involved.

I sent a letter about the rally with some background information on Disney's behavior to each middle school family (we have only 36 kids) and requested that anyone who was interested join me on the first Saturday of protest, Dec. 7, 1996.

Most of the responses were positive. One parent phoned to say that even though she and her daughter would be away during that weekend, she appreciated my organizing the parents and students; three more parents pledged to attend; two other parents took me up on my offer to transport students.

Not everyone was pleased. Soon after the letter was mailed, two of my colleagues and friends felt I'd sealed my fate and would be fired. Although I'd paid for the mailing, they reasoned that involving the school community in political activity, even in an indirect way, would be a direct challenge to the director's admonition from the previous school year. They feared the fallout resulting from my termination would hurt the school's reputation. Another co-worker told me that her boyfriend, a superintendent of schools in another country, had seen the letter (her son is a student of mine) and remarked that if I'd worked for him, he would have had my head on a platter. Two parents felt I'd abandoned my role as a neutral educator by leading students to protest. They were worried that I hadn't presented both sides of the story.

By putting social action at the center of learning, we join those who challenge injustice in our schools and in our communities.

What are the two sides when people working in factories contracted by American corporations in Asia and Central America don't earn enough to feed their families, are routinely beaten and abused, and have no legal options to remedy their situation? Balance and other perspectives have their utility, but I completely eschew moral relativism. It's one thing to strive for balance (and we should) by teaching, for example, that no civilization or religion has a corner on superiority. It's likewise important to present as valid other perspectives, such as those of indigenous populations, women, and other groups whose stories are often marginalized and distorted by traditional accounts. But certain issues do not have two equally valid sides.

We don't teach the civil rights movement by equating the views of the Bull Connors of the South with the views of Rosa Parks and Martin Luther King, Jr. And we don't teach the Holocaust by presenting the Nazi viewpoint as anything other than evil. Why should our approach to the issue of American companies using sweatshop labor be any different?

I believe educators, parents, and students have a responsibility to expose injustice and oppression, and the call for "balance" can be used to cloud the real issues. Why shouldn't we be forced to look outside our proverbial windows and help make the world a better place?

Outside the Disney Store

Two students initially joined me in the protest outside the Disney Store in downtown San Francisco on a cold, blustery Saturday morning nearly three weeks before Christmas in 1996. The two students, Jessica Whyman and Natalie Shamash, and I handed out leaflets and asked for signatures on petitions to Michael Eisner. We held placards that said, "Boycott Disney" and "Disney Supports the Repression of Workers in Central America."

Throngs of shoppers and tourists crowded the streets in search of the latest bargain or the perfect gift, but amid the din of holiday traffic, we felt invisible. Many people passed us with blank stares, few words, and the look of indifference.

Jessica and Natalie were becoming chilled and disillusioned but their mood changed dramatically after Lizzie arrived. While none of the other students had ever attended a "formal" protest before, Lizzie had experience at political gatherings. Two years ago, for instance, she and her father, Jerry, had gone to Washington as part of an OXFAM [Oxford Committee for Famine Relief]-sponsored youth meeting to pressure President Bill Clinton on meaningful aid to those ravaged by war and famine in Africa. Lizzie had also won OXFAM's postcard-drawing contest and had spoken at several functions as a result.

Lizzie's presence re-energized Jessica and Natalie. People started talking to us, mostly to the three of them, and signing our petitions. Before long we were joined by Lizzie's father, two more of my students, Samantha and Ian, and their mother, Pam. By noon, our kernel of eight had grown into a crowd of nearly 75 protesters, including members of the Bay Area Haitian-American Council, political activists, several local union representatives, and members of a local Unitarian Meeting House. There was also a group of striking workers, mostly Latina women, who had walked out against a Disney licensee over unfair working conditions, intimidation, and discrimination.

What happened when I returned to school on Monday? Luckily, not much. Colleagues who feared there would be repercussions, such as my getting fired, were wrong. As it turned out, the director's only stated concern was whether I'd improperly used the school directory for the mailing to parents telling them about the protest. The school guarantees that the directory will not be used for business or non-profit purposes, and he was worried that someone might accuse the school of violating that binding agreement.

For my part, I know we did the right thing by attending the rally, just as I know that teaching for social justice is critical to every classroom. By putting social action at the center of learning, we join those who challenge injustice in our schools and in our communities.

Organizations to Contact

The editors have compiled the following list of organizations concerned with the issues debated in this book. The descriptions are derived from materials provided by the organizations. All have publications or information available for interested readers. The list was compiled on the date of publication of the present volume; the information provided here may change. Be aware that many organizations take several weeks or longer to respond to inquiries, so allow as much time as possible.

American Federation of Labor–Congress of Industrial Organizations (AFL-CIO)
815 16th St. NW, Washington, DC 20006
(202) 637-5000 • fax: (202) 637-5058
web address: http://www.aflcio.org

The AFL-CIO is a federation of national and local labor unions. Its goal is to improve the lives of working families and to bring economic justice to the workplace. The federation organizes labor unions and lobbies for policy changes; likewise, its various committees and departments conduct research and education services for unions. It publishes the weekly newsletter *Work in Progress*.

Children's Rights Information Network (CRIN)
c/o Save the Children
17 Grove Ln.
London SE5 8RD, UNITED KINGDOM
Tel +44-171-703-5400 • fax: +44-171-793-7626
e-mail: crin@pro-net.co.uk • web address: http://www.crin.ch

CRIN is an international network of children's rights organizations that supports the effective exchange of information about children and their rights to help implement the United Nations Convention on the Rights of the Child. The network publishes information on children's rights, including *Towards Transnational Cooperation for Children* and *The Moral Status of Children: Essays on the Rights of the Child*.

Corporate Watch
PO Box 29344, San Francisco, CA 94129
(415) 561-6568 • fax: (415) 561-6493
e-mail: corpwatch@igc.org • web address: http://www.corpwatch.org

Corporate Watch serves as an on-line magazine and resource center for investigating and analyzing corporate activity. Past articles have included "Blood Sweat and Shears: Can We Put an End to Sweatshops?" as well as news and action alerts. Its editors are committed to documenting the social, political, economic, and environmental misdeeds committed by corporations and building support for human rights, environmental justice, and democratic control over corporations. Corporate Watch is a project of the Transnational Resource and Action Center, which works to educate people about the social and environmental impact of corporate globalization.

Human Rights Watch
350 Fifth Ave., New York, NY 10118-3299
(212) 290-4700
e-mail: hrwnyc@hrw.org • web address: http://www.hrw.org

Human Rights Watch is an activist organization dedicated to protecting the human rights of people around the world, including workers' rights. It investigates and exposes human rights violations and holds abusers accountable. It publishes an annual world report, and its Children's Rights Project has published *The Small Hands of Slavery: Bonded Child Labor in India* and *Children's Rights and the Rule of Law.*

National Consumers League (NCL)
1701 K St. NW, Suite 1201, Washington, DC 20006
(202) 835-3323 • fax: (202) 835-0747
web address: http://www.nclnet.org

NCL works to protect and promote the economic and social interests of America's consumers through education, investigation, and research. Its members want to ensure that goods are produced under fair, safe, and healthy working conditions that foster quality products for consumers and a decent standard of living for workers. NCL worked for the first minimum wage laws, overtime compensation, and the child labor provisions in the Fair Labor Standards Act. The league publishes various articles on U.S. and international child labor and the newsletter *NCL Bulletin*, printed six times a year.

National Labor Committee
275 Seventh Ave., 15th Fl., New York, NY 10001
(212) 242-3002
web address: http://www.nlcnet.org

The committee seeks to educate and actively engage the U.S. public on human and labor rights abuses by corporations. Through education and activism, it works to end labor and human rights violations, ensure a living wage, and help workers and their families live and work with dignity. Its report *Made in China: Behind the Label* details Chinese sweatshops, and its video *Zoned for Slavery: The Child Behind the Label* deals with child labor in Central America.

Union of Needletrades, Industrial, and Textile Employees (UNITE)
1710 Broadway, New York, NY 10019
(212) 265-7000
e-mail: StopSweatshops@uniteunion.org
web address: http://www.uniteunion.org/

UNITE is an apparel and textile workers' union that fights for workers' rights in several industries. Its website includes updates on activists' accomplishments, news reports on labor legislation, and information about UNITE's Stop Sweatshops campaign.

United Nations Children's Fund (UNICEF)
U.S. Committee
333 E. 38th St., New York, NY 10016
(212) 686-5522 • fax: (212) 779-1679
e-mail: information@unicefusa.org
web address: http://www.unicef.org • http://www.unicefusa.org

The United States is one of thirty-seven nations that raises money for UNICEF, an organization that provides health care, clean water, improved nutrition, and education to millions of children in more than 160 countries and territories. UNICEF also works to spread awareness about the status of the world's children. Its publications include *The State of the World's Children 1997* and presentation papers from international child labor conferences.

U.S. Department of Labor
Bureau of International Labor Affairs (ILAB)
200 Constitution Ave. NW, Room S-2235, Washington, DC 20210
(202) 219-6061
web address: http://www.dol.gov/dol/ilab

ILAB carries out the Department of Labor's international responsibilities and assists in formulating the international economic, trade, and immigration policies that affect American workers. Its reports on child labor include the two-volume *By the Sweat and Toil of Children* and *The Apparel Industry and Codes of Conduct: A Solution to the International Child Labor Problem?*

Bibliography

Books

Philip Alston, ed. — *The Best Interests of the Child: Reconciling Culture and Human Rights.* New York: Oxford University Press, 1994.

Maggie Black — *In the Twilight Zone: Child Workers in the Hotel, Tourism, and Catering Industry.* Geneva, Switzerland: International Labour Office, 1995.

Ryszard Cholewinski — *Migrant Workers in International Human Rights Law: Their Protection in Countries of Employment.* New York: Oxford University Press, 1997.

Deon Filmer and Lant Pritchett — *Environmental Degradation and the Demand for Children: Searching for the Vicious Circle.* Washington, DC: World Bank, Policy Research Department, Poverty and Human Resources Division, 1996.

Russell Freedman and Lewis Hine — *Kids at Work: Lewis Hine and the Crusade Against Child Labor.* New York: Clarion Books, 1998.

Kathlyn Gay — *Child Labor: A Global Travesty.* Brookfield, CT: Millbrook Press, 1998.

Human Rights Watch — *Corporations and Human Rights: Freedom of Association in a Maquila in Guatemala.* New York: Human Rights Watch, 1997.

Human Rights Watch/Asia — *Rape for Profit: Trafficking of Nepali Girls and Women to India's Brothels.* New York: Human Rights Watch, 1995.

Human Rights Watch/Children's Rights Project — *The Small Hands of Slavery: Bonded Child Labor in India.* New York: Human Rights Watch, 1996.

Maureen E. Jaffe et al. — *By the Sweat and Toil of Children: The Use of Child Labor in U.S. Agricultural Imports and Forced and Bonded Child Labor.* Upland, PA: Diane, 1997.

Susan Kuklin — *Iqbal Masih and the Crusaders Against Child Slavery.* New York: Henry Holt, 1998.

Michael Lavalette — *Child Employment in the Capitalist Labour Market.* Brookfield, VT: Avebury, 1994.

Gary P. Leupp — *Servants, Shophands, and Laborers in the Cities of Tokugawa, Japan.* Princeton, NJ: Princeton University Press, 1992.

Juliet H. Mofford, ed. — *Child Labor in America.* Carlisle, MA: Discovery Enterprises, 1997.

Mohd. Mustafa   *Child Labor in India: A Bitter Truth.* New Delhi, India: Deep & Deep, 1996.

Olga Nieuwenhuys   *Children's Lifeworlds: Gender, Welfare, and Labour in the Developing World.* New York: Routledge, 1994.

Jemera Rone   *Children in Sudan: Slaves, Street Children, and Child Soldiers.* New York: Human Rights Watch, 1995.

Sonia A. Rosen,   *The Apparel Industry and Codes of Conduct: A Solution to*
Maureen Jaffe, and   *the International Child Labor Problems.* Upland, PA: Diane,
Jorge Perez-Lopez   1997.

Andrew Ross   *No Sweat: Fashion, Free Trade, and the Rights of Garment Workers.* New York: Verso, 1997.

Richard L. Siegel   *Employment and Human Rights: The International Dimension.* Philadelphia: University of Pennsylvania Press, 1994.

Darryl M. Trimiew   *God Bless the Child That's Got Its Own: The Economic Rights Debate.* Atlanta: Scholars Press, 1997.

Periodicals

Skip Barry   "Taking Aim at Child Slavery," *Dollars and Sense*, July/August 1997.

Aaron Bernstein   "A Potent Weapon in the War Against Sweatshops," *Business Week*, December 1, 1997.

Marc Breslow   "Crimes of Fashion: Those Who Suffer to Bring You Gap T-Shirts," *Dollars and Sense*, November/December 1995.

Economist   "Central America Opens for Business," June 21, 1997.

Economist   "Stamping Out Sweatshops: Dress Code," April 19, 1997.

Charles Fairchild   "How to Get Cheap Shoes in a Global Economy: The Sweatshops' Media Spin Doctors," *Against the Current*, July/August 1997.

Mary Rose Fernandez   "Commodified Women," *Peace Review*, September 1997.

Sean M. Fitzgerald   "Barbie Talks Back," *Humanist*, July/August 1997.

Anton Foek   "Sweatshop Barbie: Exploitation of Third World Labor," *Humanist*, January/February 1997.

Steven Greenhouse   "A New Approach to Eliminating Sweatshops," *New York Times*, April 13, 1997.

Pharis J. Harvey   "The Scourge of Child Labor," *Christian Social Action*, March 1997. Available from 100 Maryland Ave. NE, Washington, DC 20002.

Bob Herbert   "A Good Start," *New York Times*, April 14, 1997.

William J. Holstein   "Santa's Sweatshop," *U.S. News & World Report*,
et al.   December 16, 1996.

Rob Howe,   "Kathie Lee Gifford Learns the Hard Way That Sweat-
Liz McNeil,   shops Are Flourishing Again in American Cities," *People*,
and Ron Arias   December 10, 1996.

Issues and Controversies on File	"Sweatshops," March 7, 1997. Available from Facts on File News Service, 11 Penn Plaza, New York, NY 10001-2006.
Siu Hin Lee and Celeste Mitchell	"Sweat Shop Workers Struggle in New York's Chinatown," *Z Magazine*, February 1998.
JoAnn Lum	"Sweatshops Are Us," *Dollars and Sense*, September 19, 1997.
Abigail McCarthy	"Kinder, Gentler Sweatshops," *Commonweal*, June 6, 1997.
Barbara McClatchie-Andrews	"Holes in Their Shoes: Nicaragua's Army of Working Children," *World & I*, June 1, 1997. Available from 3600 New York Ave. NE, Washington, DC 20002.
Pradeep S. Mehta	"Cashing in on Child Labor," *Multinational Monitor*, April 1994.
David Moberg	"Childhood's End: Child Labor Indicts the Global Marketplace," *In These Times*, June 14, 1998.
David Moberg	"The Global Labor Cop," *In These Times*, July 22, 1996.
Jo-Ann Mort	"Immigrant Dreams: Sweatshop Workers Speak," *Dissent*, Fall 1996.
Keith B. Richburg and Anne Swardson	"Sweatshops or Economic Development?" *Washington Post National Weekly Edition*, August 5–11, 1996. Available from Reprints, 1150 15th St. NW, Washington, DC 20071.
Larry Salomon	"Sweatshops in the Spotlight," *Third Force*, September/October 1996.
Mark Schapiro and Trudie Styler	"Children of a Lesser God," *Harper's Bazaar*, April 1, 1996.
Robert A. Senser	"To End Sweatshops," *Commonweal*, July 18, 1997.
Myron Weiner	"Children in Labor: How Sociocultural Values Support Child Labor," *World & I*, February 1, 1995.
David L. Wilson	"Do Maquiladoras Matter?" *Monthly Review*, October 1, 1997.

Index

102